The Origins of the Bible:
The Facts and Fiction Behind
the World's Greatest Book

ISBN 1-58898-695-0

The Origins of the Bible:
The Facts and Fiction Behind the World's Greatest Book

Samuel Graham

Global Book Publisher
North Charleston, South Carolina

Title No. 695
2002

The Origins of the Bible: The Facts and Fiction Behind the World's Greatest Book

Contents

Introduction

Where did the Bible of the Judeo-Christian tradition come from? Many Bible readers have only a hazy notion regarding this question. While the reader may be aware that the Bible was not carried down from Mount Sinai by Moses along with the Ten Commandments, there are many surprising facts about the Bible that seldom filter down to the average parishioner from the theological seminaries. This book discloses many of those facts.

One of the fundamental characteristics of human society is the tendency for tradition to sprout and grow up alongside the facts of history. Social, political and religious forces frequently work together to create erroneous religious beliefs. Those beliefs gradually mature over the centuries into traditions. Only by constantly sifting through information from different sources and backgrounds can a person hope to separate fact from fiction. The serious Bible student has the difficult decision of whether or not to accept historical facts regardless of the truths they may reveal.

The beginnings of the Bible stretch back 3,500 years to a time for which there is precious little information. From that time forward the volume of historical records slowly grows. As a result, there is much more known about the formation of the New Testament than there is the Old Testament. In spite of this fact, there is just as much speculative religious tradition surrounding the New Testament as there is the Old Testament.

The ultimate goal of most Bible readers is to determine what God expects from them in this life. In order to fulfill this goal it is necessary to understand the nature and purpose of the writings that are collectively called the Bible. This cannot be done until it is understood where these writings came from and who decided to compile them into a book. All orthodox Jews and Christians believe that God played a vital role in the formation of the Bible, and so the search for the Bible's origins should begin with the most fundamental of all questions: Is there a God? If there is not enough evidence to support the belief in God, then the purpose of this book would be reduced to mere historical and literary curiosity, and nothing more. Once the textual nature of the Bible has been determined, this information can be correlated with biblical hermeneutics and the process of exegesis can then begin.

In dedication to blood and platelet donors everywhere who give their time and effort that others might live.

Chapter One

The Existence of God

Nicolaus Copernicus published a book in 1543 that describes the heliocentric theory of the solar system. This theory states that the planets of the solar system, including the earth, revolve around the sun. While this is a well-known fact today, even to schoolchildren, back in the 16th century this theory was considered religious heresy by virtually everyone. In that day the geocentric theory, which stated that the sun and planets revolved around the earth, was considered to be a biblical truth. This theory dates back in antiquity at least as far as Aristotle, and was supported by the astronomer Claudius Ptolemy in the 2nd century of our era. According to the Protestant reformer Martin Luther, Copernicus was "a fool who wishes to reverse the entire science of astronomy, but sacred Scripture tells us that Joshua commanded the sun to stand still, not the earth."[1] Another reformer, John Calvin, asked, "Who will venture to place the authority of Copernicus above that of the Holy Spirit?"[2] The Jesuits accused Copernicus of promoting a heresy "more scandalous, more detestable, and more pernicious to Christianity than any contained in the books of Calvin, of Luther, and of all other heretics put together,"[3] and the Catholic Church published the following historic edict in 1616:

> The view that the sun stands motionless at the center
> of the universe is foolish, philosophically false, and

utterly heretical, because contrary to Holy Scripture. The view that the earth is not the center of the universe and even has a daily rotation is philosophically false, and at least an erroneous belief."[4]

Two scientists, Kepler and Galileo, continued the search for the facts of astronomy in the 17th century, both publishing books defending the heliocentric theory. Galileo's book was placed on the Catholic's Index of Prohibited Books until 1822.

Copernicus lived in a time when Western Civilization was beginning to emerge from the Middle Ages, a time when knowledge and learning was suppressed by Christian dogma. With the beginning of the Age of Enlightenment the hold that Christian traditions had on the minds of men and women began to slip. One man's invention played a monumental role in this new quest for knowledge. Gutenberg's printing press, which began printing books in the mid-15th century, made possible the dissemination of information on a grand scale. Thereafter information was available to everyone and not just the clergy. Some of the first published religious texts made available to the public included Gutenberg's Bible, Erasmus' Greek New Testament, and Luther's German Bible.

Copernicus' book demonstrated that things are not always as they first appear to be. The sun appears to travel across the sky. The world appears to be flat. A stick half submerged in a pool of water appears to be bent. The discoveries made in the realm of physics in the 20th century that prove the world is not always as it seems are still beyond comprehension to most people. The truths of science are not always apparent to the senses. Scientists are discovering the true nature of matter with the help of scientific inventions such as telescopes of different kinds, bubble chambers, and particle accelerators. Material objects appear to be solid, but in reality they are composed of mostly empty space. If an atom were enlarged to the size of a football stadium, the nucleus would be a basketball at the center of the stadium and the electrons would be golf balls circling the stadium above the last row of seats.

The human body is mostly empty space, but because human eyesight is so poor the elementary particles of matter cannot be seen. Thus people appear to have solid bodies. There is so much empty space in the human body that as the reader sits reading this book there are millions of particles called neutrinos that are passing through him or her, and through the earth as well. The sun produces these neutrinos as a by-product of its nuclear fusion. They are among the smallest of all atomic particles and they could be pictured as grains of sand passing through the football stadium between the golf balls and the basketball. Even lead, the densest of the elements, is mostly empty space. If all the empty space was to be removed from every atom of the sun, which is hundreds of thousands of miles in diameter, the resulting body of matter would only be a couple miles across. This actually takes place in nature whenever a star uses up all of its nuclear fuel. The star collapses under the force of its own gravitational field to form a white dwarf, a neutron star, or a black hole, depending on the size of the star before it collapses. A star that is twice the size of the sun will some day collapse onto itself and become a black hole that is so dense that nothing, including light, can escape its gravitational field. Thus it would appear as a black circle to anyone peering at it through a telescope. Atoms would be crushed beyond recognition in a black hole.

Subatomic particles themselves are not solid objects but are fuzzy shapeless fields of energy that defy description. Matter is nothing more than a form of energy as Einstein discovered with his famous equation $e=mc2$. There are billions of galaxies in the universe, each one containing billions of stars. Each star is billions of tons in mass, and each pound of mass contains billions of atoms. This is reality. There are undoubtedly some who cannot accept such a bizarre description of the world, just as the world could not at one time accept the heliocentric theory of the solar system. There are also many people today who occupy the two extremes of the philosophical spectrum: Bible students who refuse to relinquish religious beliefs when they are found to contradict historical facts, and atheists who refuse to accept the scientific evidence for the existence of God.

The scientists who are atheists have decided that this material universe is the extent of existence; there is nothing more. If something cannot be seen under a microscope then it does not exist. This is not a scientific or logical conclusion, but a philosophical one. Science does not doubt the existence of subatomic particles, yet by scientific definition it is impossible to isolate and observe one of these particles. They are assumed to exist because their "tracks" can be observed in bubble chambers and in particle accelerators. Likewise, no one will ever be able to observe God with scientific instruments, but his "tracks" can be seen throughout the universe in the design of complex physical laws and especially in the design and beauty of life on this planet.

Thoughts, ideas, and mental pictures cannot be seen under a microscope or physically detected in any other way, but that does not preclude their existence. If there is no metaphysical mind or spirit, then what is called intelligence is nothing more than the mathematical algorithms of atomic particles colliding with one another. Everything in the universe, including people's thoughts, could then be traced back to the happenstance collisions of atoms under the influence of electromagnetism and gravity. There would be no free will in such a universe because every thought would simply be the pre-determined result of atoms mathematically obeying the forces of nature. One of the eminent physicists of this age, Roger Penrose, admits in his book *Shadows of the Mind* that the laws of physics cannot at this time explain the existence of thoughts. In truth, it appears that the laws of physics will never explain the spiritual side of life. The material universe cannot create immaterial thoughts and ideas. Dumb atoms obeying the law of physics cannot produce intelligence. It would appear that the human mind belongs in the immaterial, metaphysical realm—the realm of God.

Outside of the fact that God, along with sub-atomic particles, cannot be seen, there is *no credible evidence* that God does not exist. The evidence points in the opposite direction.

The mathematical probability that the universe and life on earth came into existence by chance is next to none. The physical laws of the universe create a perfect equilibrium between matter and gravity that allows the formation of stars, without which there would be no life. The simplest form of life on earth has complex DNA strands and protein molecules that contain the necessary information for the life form to function. There is more information in the simplest life form than in the entire *Encyclopedia Britannica*. If there is no Creator then this means that millions of years ago, before there was life, there suddenly appeared out of nowhere on this planet a configuration of millions of molecules joined in exactly the right order to give birth to a living, reproducing life form. This life form would then have to accidentally mutate into complex biological systems. The probability of these events occurring by chance is virtually nonexistent. The only other probability remaining is that of the universe and life being created by an intelligent Creator, and that probability for all practical purposes is 100%.

Evolution is a fact. To be more precise, "micro" evolution is a fact. Geneticists have been producing new strains of plants and insects for years by altering their genetic makeup. Unfortunately, biologists lump "micro" and "macro" evolution together to make the claim that they are both fact. Man has yet to observe the evolution of one species into another, which is called "macro" evolution. There is little if any evidence to support the belief that all the species of life evolved from a microscopic organism. The fossil record does not show any species gradually evolving into another species. Instead, the geological stratum indicates that new species made their appearances on this earth suddenly and abruptly. Creation explains the fossil record much better than "macro" evolution. The theory of "macro" evolution should be called instead the "hypothesis of macro evolution;" there is not enough evidence to warrant the use of the term "theory."

The Big Bang theory of cosmology, on the other hand, does have enough evidence to warrant its status as a theory.

According to this theory, the universe began as a single point of infinite density billions of years ago before exploding into galaxies and stars. Astronomers know that the millions of galaxies in this universe are all moving away from each other at a high rate of speed. If all the galaxies could shift into reverse and retrace their paths, they would all meet at a single starting point. The background radiation which evenly pervades the universe was first predicted using a mathematical model of the Big Bang theory, and at a later time this radiation was actually discovered using very precise scientific instruments which measured the temperature of the radiation to be exactly what was predicted: three degrees Kelvin.

It is hard to imagine the entire universe contained inside a point of infinite density. This seems more like science fiction. However, there is a similarity between the Big Bang theory and black holes, which are astronomical objects of infinite density that exist throughout the universe today. Black holes were first mathematically predicted using the current laws of physics. Astronomers later found many objects in the universe such as quasars that are small in size and yet emit immense quantities of energy; these objects fit the descriptions of black holes. Science has no theory as to what caused the Big Bang or where matter and energy came from, although there are many hypotheses being floated about. People who have no trouble with including both science and religion in their philosophy know that God is the cause of the Big Bang. The book of Genesis hints at the Big Bang theory when God is recorded as saying, "let there be light," at the beginning of the creation narrative. According to the mathematical model of the Big Bang theory, the first physical manifestation of the Big Bang is light.

In 1982 some very amazing scientific experiments were carried out in a laboratory by a team of physicists headed by Alain Aspect in France. Using very sophisticated instruments, the physicists tracked particles of light, called photons, and discovered that the photons changed course in the middle of their trip through the scientific apparatus as a direct result of a particular instrument that was at the end of the experiment.

The photons somehow knew what instrument was in front of them at the end of their trip, and these particles of light took appropriate action before reaching that instrument. How could a photon "know" what conditions existed at its destination before it arrived there? The answer lies in the mathematical equations of Albert Einstein that were first published in 1905.

According to Einstein's theory of relativity, time slows down for objects as they increase in speed. This has been scientifically demonstrated over and over again in particle accelerators. If an object were to reach the speed of light, time would stop and cease to exist for that object. Einstein's equations do not allow anything with mass to reach the speed of light; first, it would take an infinite amount of energy to push an object to that speed, and second, its mass would become infinite. But photons have no mass. That is why they can travel at light speed, and that is why time does not exist for them. Photons "know" their future; they know what is waiting for them at their destination. Past, present and future are all the same to a photon.

This may sound like science fiction to the average person, but the mathematical equations of relativity theory and quantum mechanics (particle physics) make possible such modern day marvels as computer chips, lasers, nuclear reactors, satellite communication, and much more. The atheist scoffs at the notion of a God who is not confined by time, a God who had no beginning and has no end. Science, however, establishes the fact that time is a relative characteristic that only exists in a material world of "slow" moving objects. Time does not exist for light, and time does not exist for any Being outside this material universe. In this sense the biblical writer John was correct when he said, "God is light." God could not have had a beginning for the simple reason that time does not exist for him.

Time is not only mathematically relative, it is also relative according to how each person perceives it mentally. Time seems to pass more quickly for seniors than for children. Time passes more quickly when one is busy than when one is bored. When compared to eternity, any length of time is but a fleeting moment. Just as a second is seemingly instantaneous, one hundred years is instantaneous when compared to a billion trillion years. The biblical writer James wrote that life is but a mist that appears for a moment and then vanishes. Those individuals who can intellectually accept and digest the fact that this life is only seconds long when compared to eternity can greatly decrease the amount of worry in their life and better prioritize their goals. Moreover, a proper understanding of time is helpful in answering the atheist's strongest case against the belief in God: the presence of pain and suffering on earth and the Christian belief in eternal torment.

The Problem of Pain and Suffering

The world is full of pain and suffering, some of which is caused by man and some by nature. Mankind may be responsible for wars and persecution, but a great deal of suffering comes from natural causes such as tornadoes, hurricanes, floods, famine, and diseases. If God is the creator of this planet and of life, then he alone is directly responsible for the pain and suffering that comes from natural causes. God operates outside of time, and so he knew in advance of our creation that we would not only suffer from natural calamities but also from the evils committed by other people. There may be individuals who were able to use their pain and suffering to become more useful and productive to society, as pure metal is refined by the fire, but this does not explain the pain and suffering of children who die before reaching adulthood. An all-powerful God could have created a world without natural disasters and created people without the human desires and deficiencies that cause them to hurt others, while allowing them to retain their free will. For that matter, an all-powerful God did not need to create the universe or people to begin with. If God is perfect in every way, then the state of existence before creation must have been perfect, making it unnecessary for God to have created the universe or human beings. The atheist claims that a merciful and just God could and would not allow the sorrows of the world to exist. This powerful argument has always been difficult to refute.

It cannot be denied that God is directly or indirectly responsible for pain and suffering. It is not known why he created human beings, let alone why he created the ingredients for pain and suffering that exist in this world. The answer to the problem of pain and suffering lies in placing it in the proper perspective. As mentioned earlier, the metaphysical side of each person, the soul, spirit, mind, i.e., the source of one's thoughts, belongs to the timeless realm of God. Every person's mind has been wedded in some mysterious way to the four dimensions of this universe, but this marriage with matter is, relatively speaking, only seconds long. After death the mind, or spirit, returns to the timeless, eternal existence with God.

Pain and suffering is very real and sometimes horrible as it is being experienced, but it lasts but seconds when compared to the eternity of the next life. Pain itself is a very relative experience. A child's tolerance for pain is much less than that of an adult. A baby will scream bloody murder and shed crocodile tears if it gets diaper rash or does not get its bottle at the usual time. A somewhat older child will do likewise if a playmate takes away his or her toy. Adults can become seriously hurt and not initially notice the pain if they are intensely concentrating on a problem at hand. When a person leaves this physical body after death he or she will probably look back at his or her short life and realize that their sufferings were not nearly as bad as they seemed at the time. If everyone lived each day as though it were their last with the expectation of beginning eternal life tomorrow, then the true relative nature of time and of suffering would be easier to understand.

If God were a tyrant and a despot, an evil God, then the problem of pain and suffering would of course disappear. There would be no contradiction for an unjust Creator to allow suffering or to eternally torment people. If God were a merciless tyrant, one could either serve him out of fear, to hopefully escape eternal torment, or one could uphold a high moral standard and refuse to serve an evil being, regardless of the consequences. Of course, if God were an evil tyrant then his word could not be trusted because he would not be above lying to people. His threats of eternal torment could be false, along with any promises of eternal life that he might make. Hopefully everyone would refuse to serve an evil God and choose instead to ignore him.

If one is going to serve God then one must assume up front that he is a God of love, justice, and mercy. The atheist insists that a God with these attributes would never eternally torment anyone. This time the atheist may have a foolproof case. For God to allow someone to suffer in this world for a moment is one thing; to allow someone to suffer endlessly for something he or she did in a brief moment of time is something else entirely. There is no mercy, no love, and no justice in tormenting someone endlessly. If God were indeed an evil tyrant, there is nothing he could do which would be worse than eternally tormenting a person. There is no question that Hitler was a despotic tyrant, but what he did lasted but a moment compared to eternal torment. Even if the punishment of hell is softened by calling it eternal separation from God, or annihilation, rather than eternal torment, that does not change the fact that God would be punishing someone for all eternity for a sin committed in a brief moment in time.

There is simply no justice or mercy in eternal punishment of any kind. Even in the Old Testament the decreed punishments for sin are always of like kind: an eye for an eye, a physical life for a physical life. By this standard, a crime of limited duration should be met with a punishment of limited duration. Eternal punishment has no like kind. Does the atheist really have a foolproof case? Can God be both a loving, merciful God and an evil tyrant at the same time? Some people would say yes, claiming that God is so superior to human beings that they just cannot fathom his attributes of love, justice and mercy. This explanation does not wash, though, for two reasons. First, people were made in the image of God and carry the imprint of his spiritual attributes, although in many people those attributes are buried deep beneath their human attributes. Second, the Bible teaches that people are to love others because God loves them, and people are to dispense justice and mercy because God does the same. God expects people to live by his own standards. Moreover, God is so superior to human beings that he will extend his justice and mercy far beyond any degree that any person would. He is much more likely to forgive than the most forgiving person.

Fortunately, the belief in eternal punishment is based upon mistranslated words and misunderstood figurative language in the Bible. This will be fully examined later. The atheist's claim that a loving, merciful God would not eternally punish anyone is exactly right, because that would result in a contradiction of outlandish proportions. The atheist's argument regarding God's existence fades away, though, when the false belief of eternal punishment is discarded.

God's existence cannot be proved, but it is not necessary to prove his existence. Everyone makes decisions every day based upon available facts and information without having to prove that one choice is better than another. The evidence for the existence of God is so overwhelming that the atheist's belief that there is no God requires much more faith than does a person's belief in his existence.

Chapter Two

The Old Testament

There are many versions of the Bible on the shelves of the neighborhood religious bookstore. Because the Bible was written in languages other than English, it must be translated into English since few people can read Hebrew and Greek. The English language changes over the years with words acquiring different meanings and new words being added to the dictionary. The evolution of the English language makes it necessary to periodically produce a fresh Bible translation so that the Bible can be read in the form of English that is currently being spoken.

Every Bible publisher receives the Bible that it is going to print from a translator or a translation committee. The translation committee for the *New King James Version*, as an example, has translated into English a Hebrew text of the Old Testament called the Stuttgart edition of the *Biblia Hebraica*. This Hebrew text is based upon the 12th century edition of the Masoretic Text called the ben Asher text. For the New Testament the translation committee used the *Textus Receptus*, or Received Text, which is a Greek text from the 16th century. These Hebrew and Greek texts that are used by translation committees are copies of copies stretching back over a thousand years. The original documents of the Bible, the autographs, have long since been lost or destroyed.

The translation committee has a difficult task because the Hebrew of the Old Testament text and the Greek of the

New Testament text cannot be translated word for word into English due to differences in syntax and idioms. Moreover, there are many words in the Greek and Hebrew that do not have corresponding words in English. Hence the individual translators must frequently call upon their own judgment to determine the best English words to use in the translation process. Even the latest English Bible translations have mistranslated words due to the difficulty of knowing the exact definitions of words in Hebrew and Greek as they were used two or three thousand years ago.

The actual writing of the Old Testament began around 1,250 BC, about 500 years after the beginning of the Jewish people. This beginning is usually identified with Abraham, whose family came from the city of Ur in Mesopotamia, which is present day Iraq. Abraham probably belonged to a particular classification of nomads called the Habiru, from which possibly came the term Hebrews. The book of Genesis records that God made a covenant with Abraham, promising to make his offspring a great nation and to bless the nations of the earth through his seed. This covenant was sealed with the rite of circumcision, and the Hebrews were obligated to circumcise every male on the eighth day after birth. By way of keeping his promise God rescued the Hebrews, or Israelites, descendants of Abraham, from slavery in Egypt and his prophet Moses led them through the wilderness of the Sinai Peninsula to Mount Sinai.

Tradition has held that this mountain was in the southern portion of the Sinai Peninsula where the Monastery of St. Catherine's is located today, but recent archaeological discoveries made by Robert Cornuke and David Halbrook (documented in their book *In Search of The Mountain of God*) indicate that Mount Sinai is more likely to be in northwestern Saudi Arabia, where there is a mountain called Jabal al Lawz which has a blackened top. The granite boulders on this mountain are scorched, which would support the account in Exodus of lightning, thunder, and belching smoke coming from the mountain as Moses was ascending and descending it. There are archaeological remains on the mountain that correspond with other Mount Sinai events in the book of Exodus, and its location in northwestern Saudi Arabia better fits the chronology of the Exodus events than does the location of the Monastery of St. Catherine's.

It is here at Mount Sinai that Genesis records God and the Israelites entering into a treaty, or covenant. Treaties were common in that era; a superior power would confer privileges on an inferior country in return for undertaking specific obligations. The Hittites had suzerainty treaties with the countries they conquered and these treaties resemble God's treaty with the Israelites. Around the time of the Israelites' exodus from Egypt the Egyptians and Hittites signed a treaty, or covenant, of mutual non-aggression. Having been raised in the palace of Pharaoh Seti I, Moses would have been familiar with these treaties. The Greek word *diatheke* means "treaty" (it can also mean a will), and it is translated as "covenant" in the New Testament. The same Greek word translates into Latin as *testamentum*, which accounts for the designations "Old and New Testaments."

The covenant between God and Moses stipulated that God would give the Israelites a homeland, abundant crops, good health, and protection from their enemies, and in return the Israelites were to abide by the commandments that God dictated to Moses. If they failed to keep these commandments then God would abandon them to their enemies and to other physical hardships. This covenant made no mention of life after death, an issue that in fact is rarely mentioned in the Old Testament.

On Mount Sinai Moses received the Ten Commandments, or Decalogue, on two tablets of stone. After descending the mountain, Moses wrote down the legal code that God dictated to him. This legal document, God's covenant with the Israelites, is referred to in the Pentateuch, the first five books of the Bible, as the Book of the Covenant and the Book of the Law:

> When Moses went and told the people all the Lord's words and laws, they responded with one voice,

"Everything the LORD has said we will do." Moses then wrote down everything the LORD had said... Then he took the Book of the Covenant and read it to the people (Ex 24:3-7).

This Book of the Covenant was the original Bible of the Jews. There is no extant copy of the Book of the Covenant today. It is not known what language it was written in. There is no way of knowing if all the commandments from the Book of the Covenant are found in the Torah, another name for the Pentateuch. Some scholars believe that the commandments that immediately follow the Ten Commandments in Exodus chapter 20 and that continue to the end of chapter 23 represent the contents of the Book of the Covenant. Orthodox Jews have always held the Torah to be more sacred than the rest of the Old Testament because they believe that the entire Torah was dictated by God to Moses, and it is the Torah that contains the Covenant commandments of God. Jewish scholars of late antiquity organized the laws of the Covenant into a list of 613 commandments, consisting of 248 mandatory commandments and 365 prohibitive ones. In addition to the Book of the Covenant, God gave the Israelites the Ten Commandments:

The LORD wrote on these tablets what he had written before, the Ten Commandments he had proclaimed to you on the mountain, out of the fire, on the day of the assembly. And the LORD gave them to me. Then I came back down the mountain and put the tablets in the ark I had made, as the LORD commanded me, and they are there now (Dt 10:4-5).

No one knows the location of the Ark of the Covenant, if it still exists. If the ark is ever found intact, presumably the tablets of stone that God gave to Moses will be found inside. The Ten Commandments and the Book of the Covenant deserve to be called the Word of God since history records them as having been given directly from God to Moses. As for the Pentateuch and most of the Old Testament, no one knows exactly when they were written or by whom. The subject of biblical inspiration will be covered later in the book.

The Israelites believed in a sole, omnipotent God, who was not part of the world as the pagan gods were. God's dimensions were infinitely greater, and the universe was merely his creation. They believed in a God who had far more power and distance than that of any religion in antiquity. For this reason, any attempt to make an image of God would be insulting to him. The prohibition of making idols and images is at the top of the Ten Commandments.

The wording of many of the commandments in the Pentateuch is similar to the law codes of Mesopotamia, especially the Code of Hammurabi. But there are notable differences, too. The Hammurabi code places more importance on property and wealth than on human life. A murderer could be absolved of his crime with the payment of property or by substituting the life of another man. The commandments in the Pentateuch, by contrast, do not allow a murderer to escape the death penalty: "whoever sheds the blood of man, by man shall his blood be shed; for in the image of God has God made man" (Ge 9:6).

While few would dispute that Moses wrote the Book of the Covenant, as dictated by God, tradition holds that Moses wrote the entire Pentateuch. There is no indication in the Hebrew Bible as to who wrote the creation story, the flood story, and the historical sections of the Pentateuch; Moses is only credited with writing the Book of the Covenant which was apparently nothing more than a list of commandments, promises, and curses. According to the textual evidence, including content, terminology, writing styles, and repetitive duplication, it would appear that the Pentateuch is a compilation of at least four different major written sources involving numerous authors. The Documentary Hypothesis identifies the four major sources as "J" (JHWH), "E" (Elohim), "D" (Deuteronomy), and "P" (Priestly). The end of the Pentateuch records the death of Moses, and it is unlikely that Moses would have recorded the occurrence of his own death before he actually died. Moreover, since the Pentateuch records God giving Moses the Book of the Covenant, it is unlikely that these two books could be one and the same book.

God's inspiration can be seen in the writing of the creation story, which proceeds in a rational and scientific sequence. Genesis records that at the beginning of creation, the earth was "formless and empty," and God's first act was to create light. According to the Big Bang theory, the universe was an "empty and formless" singularity, and the first physical manifestation of the Big Bang was light. The creation stories of other civilizations by comparison are amusing and nonsensical. The story of Noah and the Flood has its basis in fact since there is physical evidence in Mesopotamia of a cataclysmic flood. There is secular historical evidence of a flood in cuneiform tablets found in the Palace of Sennacherib and the Palace of Asherbanipal. The Assyrians, Babylonians, and distant Sumerians all had memories of a flood.

When the book of Genesis arrives at the story of Abraham, the text becomes a true historical narrative that can be placed into the secular historical and archaeological timeline of Mesopotamia which begins with Sargon and the Old Akkadian period of 2360-2180 BC. The lawgiver Ur-Nammu and the Third Dynasty of Ur is dated around 2000 BC, and the statesman and law-codifier Hammurabi is from the period 1728- 1686 BC. Abraham belongs to the period between Ur-Nammu and Hammurabi.

The compilation and editing process of the Old Testament probably began around the time that the Jews were exiled in Babylon. The Jewish scribe Ezra undoubtedly took part in this. He would have brought the biblical scrolls from Babylon to Jerusalem as the official representative of the King of Persia. The editors of the Old Testament had many books from which they gathered information, and some of the information that was left out of the Hebrew Bible was familiar enough to Christian Jews for them to quote as Scripture. The gospel writer Matthew quotes one of the prophets as saying "He shall be called a Nazarene" (Mt 2:23), yet this statement is found nowhere in the Hebrew Bible. According to the writer John, Jesus made the remark "as the Scripture has said, streams of living water will flow from within him" (Jn 7:38), and again this quote is not found in the Old Testament. The following is a list of some of the books that the Old Testament editors used as source material while writing and compiling the books of the Old Testament:

- The Book of the Wars of the Lord (Nu 21:14).
- The Book of Jasher (Jos 10:13; 2Sa 1:18).
- The Scroll of the Regulations of the Kingship (1Sa 10:25).
- The Book of the Annals of the Kings of Israel (1Ki 4: 32,33).
- The Book of the Annals of the Kings of Judah (1Ki 14:29).
- The Book of the Annals of King David (1Ch 27:24).
- The Book of the Annals of Solomon (1Ki 11:41).
- The Records of Samuel the Seer (1Ch 29: 29).
- The Book of Gad the Seer (1Ch 29:29).
- The Book of Nathan the Prophet (1Ch 29:29; 2Ch 9:29).
- The prophecy of Ahijah, the Shilonite (2Ch 9:29).
- The Records of Shemaiah the Prophet (2Ch 12:15).
- The Records of the Prophet Iddo (2Ch 9:29, 13:22).
- The Annals of Jehu (2Ch 20:34).

The 613 commandments are scattered haphazardly throughout the historical narrative of the Pentateuch, which is an indication that there was editorial work involved in its composition. Since there is no way of knowing which of the commandments came from the Book of the Covenant, as the editors did not specify their source material for the commandments, it is reasonable to assume that many of the commandments came from other sources which the editors used after the Book of the Covenant was lost. Thus, the commandments that are considered to be cruel and unjust were probably from sources other than Moses. These commandments would include those which call for putting to death all those who curse their parents, who gather wood or perform any other work on the Sabbath, who practice sorcery or bestiality, and who offer sacrifices to other gods.

Other commandments promise death to any priest who approaches the altar before washing, or while wearing improper garments, or while drinking wine or other fermented drinks. Death is also promised to anyone other than a Levite (a member of the priestly tribe) who touches or even looks at the holy things in the tabernacle. It would be a stark contradiction for a merciful God to create commandments such as these that treat human life so lightly. On the other hand, many of the other 613 commandments could only have come from God, as we will later see.

There are no reliable historical records that are mistake free. There are a few instances in the Old Testament where erroneous historical details have probably crept into the narrative. In one example, it is recorded that God commanded King Saul to kill all the men, women, children, and infants of the Amalekites. This kind of conduct was probably standard practice for the barbaric nations of that day, but it would be a gross contradiction for God to demand butchery such as this. Perhaps more revolting is the story of the Israelites burning the towns of the Midianites and the fate of the women and children who were captured. Here are the orders that Moses supposedly gave the army officers:

> Now kill all the boys. And kill every woman who has slept with a man, but save for yourselves every girl who has never slept with a man (Nu 31:17-18).

It simply makes good sense to attribute these horrible events either to the customs of a barbaric age or to folklore rather than to a merciful God. It is one thing for God to aid the Israelites in their wars by tipping the balance in their favor, but quite another for him to command the murdering of innocent children.

Perhaps the most baffling book in the Old Testament is

that of Job, the great essay on the problem of suffering. No one knows who wrote it, where it came from, or when it was written. There are over 100 Hebrew words in it that can be found nowhere else, which has created problems for translators for thousands of years.

The Law, along with the Prophets and the Writings, constitute the three sections of the Old Testament. The Hebrew initials of these three sections form the word *Tanak*, which is the Jewish word for the Hebrew Bible. The Law section refers to the Pentateuch because it contains the 613 commandments. The third section, Writings, was not formally accepted into the Hebrew Bible until the Council of Jamnia in 70 AD. Jesus referred to the Bible as the "Law and Prophets," and rarely quoted from the Writings. Christians adopted the Hebrew Bible and appended it to their Christian Bible because the Hebrew Bible contains prophecies that are interpreted by Christians as applying to Jesus; the Hebrew Bible, though, was written by Jews and for Jews, and so will always remain a Jewish Bible. To this day the Samaritan Bible is restricted to the Pentateuch. The Samaritans may have rejected the other Old Testament books as Scripture due to the bitter schism with the Jews in Jerusalem.

The last book of the Old Testament would have been written around 400 BC, the time of the last Jewish prophet. The three-fold division of the Old Testament is believed to have been first mentioned in history by the grandson of Jeshua Ben Sira in 132 BC. Before this time there is no mention of the Old Testament as we know it today. There is a reference to the "scrolls of the law" and the "scroll of the covenant" in 1 Maccabees Chapter One which would correspond to the time period 167 BC. At this time the editing process for the Old Testament would have been complete, so 1 Maccabees probably refers to the Law section of the Old Testament, meaning the Torah or Pentateuch, and not the Book of the Covenant.

There was a period of time during the reign of King Manasseh of Judah that the scrolls of the law were missing or concealed. Manasseh reigned 55 years and was one of the most evil kings to occupy a throne anywhere. He would have undoubtedly destroyed any biblical scrolls that he laid his hands on. After King Josiah came to the throne and began to cleanse the land of pagan cults, the high priest found a scroll of the law in the temple. Some scholars believe that this scroll contained the commandments found in chapters 5-26 and chapter 28 of the book of Deuteronomy.

In the distant past of Jewish history an oral law began to grow up alongside the written laws. The oral law was a result of efforts to clarify the application of the Law of Moses with unusual problems that periodically appeared. As time went on, the oral law was believed by many Jews to have been authored by Moses and so was considered to be as inspired as the written law. This oral law was put into writing around the beginning of the 3rd century AD and is called the Mishna. The Torah (the written law) and the Mishna, together with the commentaries of Jewish sages, make up the Jewish Talmud, which was finished around AD 500.

Sometime in the 2nd or 3rd century BC the Hebrew Bible was translated into Greek for the benefit of the Greek speaking Jews in Alexandria in North Africa. This translation is known as the Septuagint, a term from the Latin word *septuaginta* meaning "seventy." It is believed that 70 Jews from Jerusalem (actually 72, representing six from each of the twelve tribes of Israel) were sent to Alexandria to complete this translation. The Septuagint includes the books that we now call the Apocrypha, and these books can be found in the Roman Catholic translations of the Bible. These books were not included in the Jewish Hebrew Bible because they were originally written in Greek rather than Hebrew, and they were written after the editing process on the Old Testament was complete.

When Christianity began in the first century most of the Greek-speaking Christian Jews and Gentiles used the Septuagint as their Bible. The Synagogue of the Freedmen included Greek-speaking Alexandrian Jews, and members of this synagogue objected to Stephen, a Greek-speaking Hellenist, preaching the gospel. They brought him before the Sanhedrin, the Jewish governing body, where he gave his defense. His biblical quotations and allusions included in his defense were based on the Septuagint. When Matthew quoted from Isaiah 7: 14 "behold a virgin shall conceive and bear a son" he was using the Septuagint Bible where the Greek word *parthenos* means "virgin." The word in the Hebrew Bible is *almah*, which simply means "young woman."

Today the Masoretic Text is the basis for translating the Old Testament from Hebrew into English. The oldest Masoretic manuscripts date back to the 9th century AD and are copies of copies that were made with unparalleled care and accuracy back to the 2nd century AD. Before this time, however, there was no formal system of copying with built-in checks and balances, and so the possibility of copyists' errors was much greater. The oldest extant Hebrew Bible writings were discovered with the Dead Sea Scrolls in 1947-48 and include fragments of all the 24 books of the Hebrew canon, except Esther, and the entire text of Isaiah. Some of these scrolls have been dated to the 2nd century BC. Some of the original written texts upon which the Old Testament is based are 1,000 years older than the Dead Sea Scrolls and 1,400 years older than the first copies made under the Masoretic tradition. Many copyists' errors and accretions can creep into a text over such a long period of time.

Perhaps the most interesting detail in the evolution of the Old Testament is that *the one book that is unreservedly qualified to be called the Word of God, the book that God verbally dictated to Moses, the Book of the Covenant, has been lost for well over 2,500 years.* Some or most of its contents are scattered piecemeal throughout the Pentateuch, buried within the historical narrative of the Israelites along with the commandments that were added later by the editors. This should not be of concern, because the rewards and punishments associated with this covenant were strictly limited to this physical life and to the theocracy of the Israelite nation. The very existence of life after death is a subject that is not discussed in any detail in the Old Testament. This is the reason why the Jewish sect of the Sadducees did not believe in life after death. The principles that are concerned with receiving rewards in the hereafter do appear in the Hebrew Bible, though, and they will be discussed later in the book.

Archaeology

The historical details of the Old Testament agree remarkably well with secular historical records and archaeological remains. There are a few internal historical discrepancies that would be expected in any ancient record, but overall the Bible is historically reliable. Archaeology not only verifies historical details in the Bible, but it helps illustrate and explain passages in the Bible, thereby improving our understanding of the Bible.

In the past critics believed that the biblical city of Nineveh was just a myth; this city has since been excavated. The Bible mentions a people called the Hittites that was also thought at one time to be a myth. The Hittites are mentioned in Genesis 15:20 as a nation that inhabited the land of Canaan. According to 1 Kings 10:29 the Hittites purchased chariots and horses from King Solomon. Uriah, the husband of Bathsheba, was a Hittite. This nation was a major force in the Middle East from 1750 BC until 1200 BC. In 1876 a British scholar by the name of A. H. Sayce found Hittite inscriptions carved on rocks in Turkey. Clay tablets were found in Turkey ten years later at a place called Boghaz-koy. Hugo Winckler examined the tablets and began his own expedition at the site in 1906. His excavations uncovered five temples, a fortified citadel and several massive sculptures. Over ten thousand clay tablets were discovered in one storeroom. One was a record of a treaty between Ramesses II and the Hittite king. Today there are secular professionals who specialize in studying Hittitology.

According to the Bible, the Israelites conquered the city of Jericho after God caused the walls of the city to fall outwards. The miraculous nature of the conquest has caused some scholars to dismiss the story and the existence of the city as myth. Over the past century four prominent archaeologists have excavated Jericho: Carl Watzinger, John Garstang, Kathleen Kenyon, and Bryant Wood. They discovered that Jericho had a system of fortifications. There was a retaining wall fifteen feet high surrounding the city, and another brick wall enclosed the rest of the city. The structures found between the two walls are consistent with Joshua's description of Rahab's living quarters (Jos 2:15). In one part of the city large piles of bricks were found at the base of both the inner and outer walls, indicating that there had been a sudden collapse of the fortifications. A well-timed earthquake could have caused this collapse.

King David is revered as the greatest of all Israelite kings, and despite his key role in Israel's history there had been no evidence outside the Bible attesting to his existence until just recently. For this reason critics questioned the existence of King David. In 1993, Dr. Avraham Biran and his team were excavating a site labeled Tell Dan, located in northern Galilee, when they discovered in the ruins the remains of a black basalt stele, or stone slab, containing Aramaic inscriptions. The stele contained thirteen lines of writing, and two of the lines included the phrases "The King of Israel" and "House of David." Dr. Biran estimated that the stele was erected about a century after the death of King David.

For many years archaeologists have searched the Dead Sea region in search of Sodom and Gomorrah. According to Genesis 14:3 they were located in the Valley of Siddim, which was the location of the Salt Sea, or Dead Sea. There are six wadies, or river valleys, that flow into the Dead Sea. Ancient cities were discovered along five of these wadies, the northern-most being Bab edh-Drha. Dr. William Albright began excavating this site in 1924, searching for Sodom and Gomorrah. In later years archaeologists discovered numerous houses and a large temple. There were huge grave sites found that revealed the city had been well populated during the early Bronze Age, around the time of Abraham. There was evidence that a massive fire had destroyed the city, which was buried under a coating of ash several feet thick. Dr. Bryant Wood stated that a fire began on the roofs of these buildings. This would match the biblical account of fire raining down from heaven onto the city. Dr. Wood suggested that the site of Bab edh-Drha is the biblical city of Sodom. Along with Sodom and Gomorrah there were three other cities mentioned in Genesis 14 in the region of the Dead Sea: Admah, Zoar, and Zeboiim. Archaeologists have discovered remnants of a total of five cities in the Dead Sea area, and these cities were covered in the same ash as Bab ed-Drha. One of the other cities, Numeria, which is believed to be Gomorrah, had seven feet of ash in some places.[5]

The story of Joseph and his rise to power in Egypt is believable in light of Egyptian records that show a Semite by the name of Yanhamu who was the Egyptian high commissioner under Pharaoh Akhentaten about the same time Joseph was in Egypt. In the next century there was a Semite called Ben Ozen who was the marshal of Pharaoh Merenptah's court. The first secular reference to Israel is found on an artifact that dates to 1220 BC, which states that Pharaoh Merenptah defeated "Israel" in a battle in Canaan. A document from the reign of Ramesses II mentions the Habiru being used to transport stones for the pharaoh.

Joshua, who had succeeded Moses as the leader of the Israelites, made a covenant with the city of Gibeon. The precise location of the city was discovered by the American archaeologist James Pritchard after the Second World War. Pritchard was able to confirm many of the biblical references to the city of Gibeon. Joshua also engaged in battle with the King of Hazor, burning and destroying his city. Hazor was excavated by the Israeli archaeologist Yigail Yadin in the 1950's, and the evidence of burning and destruction confirms the biblical record.

Prophecy

The prophecies of the Jewish prophets are detailed and have an excellent track record concerning their fulfillment.

This is an indication that these prophets received information about the future from God either through visions or inspiration. There are many long-range prophecies in the Old Testament that were fulfilled after both the Greek and Hebrew versions of the Jewish Bible were widely distributed throughout the Roman Empire, so there is no possibility of the prediction being made after the event took place. For example, Ezekiel prophesied that God would "destroy the idols and put an end to the images in Memphis." This city was the capital of ancient Egypt and according to the Greek historian Strabo, who lived around the time of Jesus, Memphis was during his lifetime a large city full of gods, temples, and statues. The prophecy had not yet been fulfilled. However, in the 7th century a Moslem army swept into Egypt and encamped not far from Memphis. This army headquarters was called Fustat, which grew over the years into present day Cairo. The population of Memphis drifted over to this new city, which used Memphis as a quarry. By the beginning of the 20th century the only relic left above ground in Memphis was a gigantic statue of Ramesses II, which has since been moved to a nearby site. Thus Ezekiel's prophecy was fulfilled. It is true that most ancient cities have been sacked and burned at least once, and many have been abandoned. But Memphis is unique in that it was stripped of nearly every stone. God had indeed "put an end to the images in Memphis."

Another part of Ezekiel's same prophecy concerns another Egyptian city, Thebes:

> This is what the Sovereign LORD says: "I will destroy the idols and put an end to the images in Memphis. No longer will there be a prince in Egypt, and I will spread fear throughout the land. I will lay waste Upper Egypt, set fire to Zoan and inflict punishment on Thebes. I will pour out my wrath on Pelusium, the stronghold of Egypt, and cut off the hordes of Thebes. I will set fire to Egypt; Pelusium will writhe in agony. Thebes will be taken by storm; Memphis will be in constant distress" (Eze 30:13-16).

Thebes was a large city and a center for pagan religions as was Memphis. God declared through Ezekiel that he would "cut off the hordes of Thebes." This city was sacked and burned several times during its history, once by Nebuchadnezzar and once by Ptolemy Lathyrus, but each time Thebes recovered. Cornelius Gallus finally destroyed the city two hundred years after Ezekiel's prophecy, thus cutting off "the hordes of Thebes" once and for all. Today the city is gone and in its place are several small villages. The ruins of Thebes are still there, including the temples and idols. Ezekiel was correct when he prophesied that Memphis would be stripped of its idols and Thebes would be "taken by storm." The population of Memphis was not "cut off"—instead they migrated to what is now Cairo, and Thebes retained its idols. God told Ezekiel exactly what would befall the populations and pagan images of both cities. Another city pair that Ezekiel prophesied about is Tyre and Sidon; both were ports on the Mediterranean about twenty miles apart:

> Therefore this is what the Sovereign LORD says: I am against you, O Tyre, and I will bring many nations against you, like the sea casting up its waves. They will destroy the walls of Tyre and pull down her towers; I will scrape away her rubble and make her a bare rock. Out in the sea she will become a place to spread fishnets, for I have spoken, declares the Sovereign LORD. She will become plunder for the nations, and her settlements on the mainland will be ravaged by the sword. Then they will know that I am the LORD.

> For this is what the Sovereign LORD says: From the north I am going to bring against Tyre Nebuchadnezzar king of Babylon, king of kings, with horses and chariots, with horsemen and a great army. He will ravage your settlements on the mainland with the sword...they will break down your walls and demolish your fine houses and throw your stones, timber and rubble into the sea. I will put an end to

your noisy songs, and the music of your harps will be
heard no more. I will make you a bare rock, and you
will become a place to spread fishnets. You will never
be rebuilt, for I the LORD have spoken, declares the
Sovereign LORD (Eze 26:3-14).

Ezekiel said that God would bring many nations against
Tyre, one of them being Nebuchadnezzar and the Babylonians
who captured the city in 573 BC. Most of the occupants moved
out to an island half a mile off the coast during the siege. The
second nation to attack Tyre was Alexander the Great in 332
BC. Because the inhabitants had remained on the island and
Alexander had no ships, he built a land bridge from the coast
to the island using the rubble from where the mainland city
had been. Alexander's workers scraped the ground bare to
get material for the bridge, thus fulfilling Ezekiel's prophecy
that God would "scrape away her rubble and make her a bare
rock...and throw your stones, timber and rubble into the sea."
With the help of foreign ships Alexander eventually captured
the island city. Over a thousand years later, in AD 1291, the
Moslems completely destroyed the city, which was never
rebuilt. Today there is a fishing village on the island that uses
the bare areas for drying their fishnets, fulfilling Ezekiel's
predictions that Tyre would "become a place to spread fishnets"
and "never be rebuilt."

The other city on the Mediterranean that Ezekiel
prophesied against was Sidon:

This is what the Sovereign LORD says: "I am against
you, O Sidon, and I will gain glory within you. They
will know that I am the LORD, when I inflict
punishment on her and show myself holy within her.
I will send a plague upon her and make blood flow
in her streets. The slain will fall within her, with the
sword against her on every side. Then they will know
that I am the LORD. No longer will the people of
Israel have malicious neighbors who are painful briers

and sharp thorns. Then they will know that I am the
Sovereign LORD (Eze 28:22-24).

Sidon has been attacked many times throughout its history
and each time the city was rebuilt. Today it is a modern Lebanese
port. Ezekiel said nothing about Sidon being totally destroyed.
Once again Ezekiel knew the unique destinies associated with
a pair of cities.

The capitals of the two great Mesopotamian empires,
Babylon and Nineveh, had their demises foretold by Israelite
prophets. Isaiah prophesied about the doom of Babylon:

> Babylon, the jewel of kingdoms, the glory of the
> Babylonians' pride, will be overthrown by God like
> Sodom and Gomorrah. She will never be inhabited
> or lived in through all generations; no Arab will pitch
> his tent there, no shepherd will rest his flocks there.
> But desert creatures will lie there, jackals will fill
> her houses; there the owls will dwell, and there the
> wild goats will leap about. Hyenas will howl in her
> strongholds, jackals in her luxurious palaces. Her time
> is at hand, and her days will not be prolonged (Isa 13:
> 19-22).

At the time of Isaiah's prophecy Babylon was the largest
city in that part of the world. Alexander the Great planned to
make Babylon the capital of his empire after he captured it in
332 BC. After Alexander's death the city's population declined
rapidly, and in the first century of our era the only inhabitants
of the site was a group of priests. Today nothing remains of
Babylon except sand and a few bricks and stones. The site
has been uninhabited for nearly two thousand years, fulfilling
Isaiah's words that "she will never be inhabited or lived in
through all generations." Grass will not grow there, confirming
Isaiah's prediction that "no shepherd will rest his flocks there."
Note that Isaiah does not predict that Babylon will be destroyed
by an invading army as was the case with Tyre and Thebes. The

prophets of Israel knew which cities God would overthrow and how they would be overthrown.

The end of Assyria's capital city, Nineveh, is foretold by Zephaniah:

> He will stretch out his hand against the north and destroy Assyria, leaving Nineveh utterly desolate and dry as the desert. Flocks and herds will lie down there, creatures of every kind. The desert owl and the screech owl will roost on her columns. Their calls will echo through the windows, rubble will be in the doorways, the beams of cedar will be exposed. This is the carefree city that lived in safety. She said to herself, "I am, and there is none besides me." What a ruin she has become, a lair for wild beasts! All who pass by her scoff and shake their fists (Zep 2:13-15).

Nineveh fell along with the Assyrian empire around 610 BC. When Zenophon and his troops passed by in 401 BC the site was desolate as predicted by Zephaniah. In our day the area is cultivated and can support flocks and herds just as Zephaniah foretold, unlike Babylon, which will never be visited by domesticated animals again. Another contrast between the two cities concerns the future habitation of those cities. Isaiah said that Babylon would never be inhabited again; this is still the case. There was no such limit placed on the future occupation of the site where Nineveh once stood. Today the suburbs of Iraq are pushing their way across Nineveh's former boundaries. Some critics point out that most ancient cities were destroyed and so it would not require God's inspiration to prophesy about their destruction. But there are many major ancient cities still occupied today, such as Damascus, Jerusalem, Aleppo, and Sidon. The Jewish prophets knew exactly which cities would be destroyed and in what manner.

Archeology and fulfilled prophecies attest to the historical reliability of the Bible. As a historical book, the Old Testament should be taken at face value regarding the recording of the miracles performed by the Jewish prophets whose credibility is strengthened by their ability to predict future events. It is safe to assume that the Creator of the universe has the ability to intervene miraculously in his creation, and so if someone performs miracles and correctly predicts the future while claiming to be God's spokesperson, then it is not unreasonable to assume that God is using that person to deliver a message to mankind.[6]

The 490 Years of Daniel

Perhaps the most amazing Jewish prophecy concerning the destruction of a city is Daniel's prophecy of the destruction of Jerusalem and its second temple, so amazing because he prophesied that it would occur exactly 490 years in the future. The city of Jerusalem figures prominently in the Hebrew Bible. Prophets foretold the destruction of Jerusalem's first temple that was built by King Solomon, the subsequent captivity of the Jews in Babylon for seventy years, and the return of the Jews to Jerusalem. Daniel begins his prophecy by stating that six events will occur by the end of the 490 years:

> Seventy "sevens" are decreed for your people and your holy city to finish transgression, to put an end to sin, to atone for wickedness, to bring in everlasting righteousness, to seal up vision and prophecy and to anoint the most holy (Da 9:24).

The term "sevens" is universally recognized by Jewish and Christian scholars alike to refer to seven-year periods. The seven-year period is significant in Jewish history because God had permitted the Jews to till the soil six years but the during seventh year the earth was to lay fallow and "rest" just as God had rested on the seventh day after creation.

Daniel divides the 490-year period into three intervals, the first being 49 years, the second being 434 years and the last interval being seven years. In verse 25 he describes the first interval of 49 years (seven weeks) as beginning with the decree to restore Jerusalem and ending with the coming of an anointed leader:

> Know therefore and vnderstand, that from the going foorth of the commandement to restore and to build Ierusalem, vnto the Messiah the Prince, shall be seuen weekes; and threescore and two weekes, the street shall be built againe, and the wall, euen in troublous times (Da 9:25 KJV first edition).

Daniel says that there will be a period of 49 years between the decree (commandment) to rebuild Jerusalem and the arrival of the Messiah the Prince. During the next 434 years (threescore and two weekes) the city will be rebuilt. The translation used above is the first edition of the *King James Version* (KJV) just as it was published in 1611, and it uses the Masoretic punctuation with a sharp break after "seuen weekes." The KJV has undergone several revisions over the years, partly to update changes in alphabet and spelling; "I" was used for "J" in the 17th century, which explains the unusual spelling for Jerusalem. In the late 19th century the punctuation in the above passage was altered in the KJV to read:

> Know therefore and understand, that from the going forth of the commandment to restore and to build Jerusalem, unto Messiah the Prince, shall be seven weeks, and threescore and two weeks: the street shall be built again...

The period between the decree and the anointed leader (Messiah the Prince) has been extended to 49 years plus 434 years, or 483 years, in the revised KJV and many modern translations. This altered reading allows for interpreting the anointed leader to be Jesus because the 483-year period would end in the first century. Jewish Bibles today still use the punctuation of the Masoretic Text, the basis for almost all Bible

translations, as does the first edition of the KJV, the RSV, the
New American Bible, and the *Good News Bible*. In the Hebrew
language the word *messiah* means "anointed one," and in the
Old Testament there are many anointed ones including kings
and high priests. God calls the Persian king Cyrus his anointed
one: "This is what the LORD says to his anointed, to Cyrus"
(Isa 45:1). According to Daniel, an anointed leader, probably
Cyrus, came to power after 49 years; the city and temple were
then rebuilt during the "threescore and two weeks," or 434
years. Daniel then predicts the second complete destruction of
Jerusalem and the temple at the end of the 434 years:

> After the sixty-two 'sevens,' the Anointed One will be
> cut off and will have nothing. The people of the ruler
> who will come will destroy the city and the sanctuary.
> The end will come like a flood: War will continue until
> the end, and desolations have been decreed (Da 9:26).

The "Anointed One," or "Messiah" in the KJV, could
refer to the high priest in Jerusalem who was killed during the
AD 66-70 war with the Romans, who destroyed the city and
temple. Daniel's last interval is a seven-year period that in the
text follows the city's destruction:

> He will confirm a covenant with many for one 'seven.'
> In the middle of the 'seven' he will put an end to
> sacrifice and offering. And on a wing of the temple
> he will set up an abomination that causes desolation,
> until the end that is decreed is poured out on him (Da
> 9:27).

This seven-year interval along with the entire 490-year
period is interpreted in many different ways among Catholics,
Protestants, and Jews. The Catholic view states that this period
of time, with the three intervals, should not be taken literally.
The Preterist view held by some Protestants and the view of
some Jews is that the 490-year period ends in AD 70 with the
second destruction of Jerusalem. This viewpoint is the most

logical since the only time the "city and the sanctuary" were destroyed after the temple's first destruction by Nebuchadezzar was when the Romans razed them in AD 70.

Perhaps the oddest interpretation is that of the Premillennialists who believe that Daniel's prophecy has "suspended time" after the first 483 years, and the final destruction of the city and the last seven years has not yet begun. According to this view, the seven-year period represents the "tribulation period" which will begin sometime in our future. Very specific time periods are indicated in Daniel's prophecy, and it is not likely that he would leave out unmentioned a 2,000-year gap between the 69th and 70th week. It is also unlikely that Daniel would not mention the second temple destruction of AD 70, of which Jesus himself prophesied.

If the city and temple were destroyed immediately after the 434-year period, then to what does the seven-year period that follows refer? In this period Daniel prophesied that a ruler would make or confirm a covenant at the beginning of the seven years and then in the middle of the interval, i.e., three and one half years, he would put an end to temple sacrifices. There is no historical evidence that these events took place just prior to the second temple destruction. The sacrifices are brought to a halt just prior to AD 70, but this is done by the Jewish Zealots, not the Romans.

According to Josephus, the famous Jewish historian of the first century, around 171 BC the ruler Antiochus Epiphanes made a covenant with the Jews, later broke that covenant and put a stop to sacrifices in the temple for three and one half years. 1 Maccabees confirms that the ruler "spoke to them deceitfully in peaceful terms, and won their trust" before attacking Jerusalem. Antiochus then put a statue of the Greek Zeus Olympios in the temple that the Jews referred to as the "abomination of desolation," using a Hebrew play-on-words. Daniel's foretelling of the "abomination of desolation" could be applied to both this event and the destruction of the temple in AD 70 when the Romans brought their pagan standards into the temple, since Jesus also prophesied about the "abomination of desolation" as an event that was to occur in his near future.

These events perfectly fulfill Daniel's seven-week interval, but they occurred 240 years before AD 70. Apparently this third interval was not originally intended to be the last sequential interval in the 490-year period. The original text of the book of Daniel was probably altered either during the editing process of the Old Testament or during the centuries of text copying. There is a problem with correlating Daniel's 490-year period with the secular historical date of the first temple destruction in 587 BC, but this may be due to the fact that the secular dates before the common era are based on the 2nd century AD astronomer Ptolemy's questionable dating system using eclipses of the moon.

During the period 166-164 BC, Judas the Maccabee, the "Hammer," and his four brothers led a guerrilla campaign and drove all the Greeks from Jerusalem. They then rededicated the temple at a solemn service that the Jews still celebrate today during the Feast of Hanukkah, or Purification. This could be the fulfillment of Daniel's sixth event, the "anointing of the most holy." Many believe this refers to the anointing of Jesus. A better translation of the sixth event is found in the *New American Bible*: "a most holy will be anointed." Even more clear is the *Good News Bible*: "and the holy Temple will be rededicated." The Hebrew word for "most holy" almost always refers to an object such as the altar or the temple rather than a person. After the "abomination of desolation" was removed by the Maccabees, the temple was anointed during the rededication service.

Considering Daniel's success at foretelling events in such detail hundreds of years before they occurred, his claim that he received his prophetic vision from an angel of God should be accepted at face value.

Microbiology and the Bible

Although Galileo was primarily an astronomer, he also

built one of the first microscopes, about the year 1610. Galileo made no discoveries with his microscope. The first discoveries were made in the 17th century by Robert Hooke, a Curator of the Royal Society of London, and by Anton van Leeuwenhoek who built microscopes as a hobby. Leeuwenhoek sent his observations to the British Royal Society. These observations included descriptions of protozoa, bacteria, and fungi. The scientists of this century did not associate the creatures found under their microscopes with disease; it was two centuries later that Robert Koch linked a particular bacteria with anthrax, the deadly disease which has been used as a biological weapon by modern-day terrorists. Viruses were not directly observed until just 50 years ago with the invention of the electron microscope.

There is no evidence in historical records before the 17th century that mankind was aware of the fact that microorganisms caused disease; otherwise the plagues that periodically swept across the world could possibly have been avoided. The bubonic plague of medieval Europe by itself wiped out one third of Europe's population. There is, however, one notable exception in ancient history where a nation had detailed information concerning how to avoid not just one particular disease, but nearly all diseases known to man. The Old Testament contains laws regarding diet, agriculture, and health practices. These laws are found in Leviticus, the third book of the Pentateuch.

God's commandments regarding the diet of the Israelites divided animal life into two basic groups, "clean" and "unclean." The "clean" animals that the Israelites were permitted to eat included cattle, sheep, goats, and deer. These animals had split hoofs and were cud-chewers. The Israelites were also permitted to eat fish that had scales and fins, and some birds. Among the "unclean" animals were those that did not have the aforementioned characteristics of split hoofs and cud-chewing such as camels, horses, and swine. Other animals considered "unclean" included the following:

• animals with paws such as dogs and cats

- marine creatures that do not have fins and scales (catfish, shrimp, crab, and lobster)
- birds of prey (owls, hawks, falcons, and eagles)
- amphibians and reptiles (lizards, frogs, snakes, and turtles)
- rodents (rats, mice, and rabbits)

Not only were the Israelites not permitted to eat "unclean" animals, they were not even permitted to touch the carcasses of these animals. At first glance these regulations appear to be nothing more than strange religious practices with no practical value. Modern day science, however, reveals that the author of these ancient regulations must have had a thorough knowledge of microbiology. Every one of the "unclean" animal groups is highly likely to pass on diseases to man through the eating of poorly cooked meat or by touching a carcass. For example, nearly all of the "unclean" animals are scavengers or bottom feeders. Swine and dogs have frequent contact with excreta. Anyone who eats poorly cooked meat from swine can contract tapeworm, erysipelas, or trichinosis.

The "unclean" marine animals are found in relatively shallow waters which city folk use for the removal of raw sewage. Shellfish absorb non-biodegradable products and heavy metals that they pass on up the food chain to humans. Rodents such as rats can transmit bubonic plague, tapeworms, ratbite fever, and rabies to people. Birds of prey can pass on these same diseases to us because a major part of their diet is rodents. The same applies to cats that hunt for their food, which is usually mice and rats. Turtles and reptiles are frequently captured in stagnant water or contaminated rivers, and are sometimes a source of Salmonella poisoning. The author of these dietary regulations was aware of a deadly connection between "unclean" animals and people which mankind did not know of until the 20th century. The Bible records God saying,

> If you pay attention to these laws and are careful to follow them, then the LORD your God will keep his covenant of love with you, as he swore to your

forefathers....The LORD will keep you free from every disease (Dt 7:12,15).

Here is another regulation that would make no sense to a primitive people, especially one with no knowledge of modern agriculture:

> For six years sow your fields, and for six years prune your vineyards and gather their crops. But in the seventh year the land is to have a sabbath of rest, a sabbath to the LORD. Do not sow your fields or prune your vineyards (Lev 25:3-4).

By planting the same crop year after year, the Israelite farmer runs the risk of allowing plant diseases, usually fungi, to infest his crops. When the farmer obeys the biblical command and allows his field to lie fallow for a year, he breaks the cycle of the plant disease, which finds it very difficult to survive a year in the soil without the host crop. The following year the farmer experiences a disease free crop. This is a primitive form of crop rotation that allows wild plants and weeds to grow in the field in place of the crop one year out of every seven. Once again the Bible seems to be aware of the presence of microorganisms and a way of avoiding them, this time in the plant kingdom.

The spreading of disease with unwashed hands, i.e., a person touching a diseased person, living or dead, and then touching another person, was a common occurrence before the 20th century. Thousands of people died in hospitals of diseases spread by unwashed hands until Dr. Semmelweis in the 19th century determined that the washing of hands prevented disease from spreading from an infected person to another patient. Yet this principle was practiced by the Israelites 3,200 years ago. According to the Bible, God's regulations include washing one's clothes and personal effects after touching the carcass of a dead person or animal. While a contaminated bronze cooking pot was to be thoroughly washed, contaminated clay pots were to be broken. Many microorganisms are nearly impossible to eradicate from porous clay vessels. Either these are nothing more than amazing coincidences, or God is the author of these biblical regulations.

Circumcision was the sign of the covenant that God made with Abraham, and later this ritual was included as one of the commandments in the Torah. Many of the Gentile nations considered this practice to be barbaric. However, S.I. McMillen reported in his book, *None of these Diseases,* that statistics show that women whose husbands were circumcised very rarely contracted cervical cancer. The bacteria Mycobacterium smegmatis grows prolifically under the foreskin of uncircumcised males. [7]

The conclusion can be drawn that God is the author of many of the commandments in the Pentateuch because only he would have had the immense scientific knowledge to formulate those commandments. These particular commandments were undoubtedly from the Book of the Covenant, which was dictated from God to Moses. The fulfilled prophecies that have been examined in detail offer credible evidence that God had sent many prophets to the Israelites. The books of the Old Testament are as historically reliable as any secular historical documents of antiquity. While there is no reason not to accept the fact that the Ten Commandments and the Book of the Covenant were dictated by God to Moses, there is no evidence within the Old Testament itself to substantiate the belief in the word-for-word inspiration of the Old Testament. For God to inspire someone to write a book does not mean that the resulting book will be error free. There is a difference between inspiration and dictation. The meaning of inspiration and how it relates to the Bible will be discussed in a later chapter.

Chapter Three

The New Testament

The city of Jerusalem, including the temple, was thoroughly destroyed in 587 BC and again in AD 70. These were watershed events for the Jewish people. The first destruction prompted the beginning of synagogue worship and the compilation and editing of the Old Testament. At the beginning of the first century of the common era Palestine and Jerusalem were ruled by the Roman Empire. During this time a Jew by the name of Jesus began preaching throughout the Judean countryside that God had sent him to bring repentance and redemption to the world of Jews and Gentiles.

According to the first four books of the New Testament, the historical records of the life of Jesus, he performed miracles and preached repentance towards God and love for one's fellow man. Jesus prophesied about the second destruction of Jerusalem that occurred in AD 70 and about his own crucifixion and resurrection that took place around AD 30. The skeptics of that time did not dispute the fact that Jesus did miracles; instead they insisted that he did so by the power of Satan. The followers of Jesus claimed that he rose from the dead, just as he said he would, and met with them several times over a period of forty days.

The event of the resurrection is the foundation of the Christian religion. If the resurrection had not occurred, Jesus' disciples would have returned to their former way of life and religion. When Jesus was arrested his disciples fled the scene. After his death one of the disciples was recorded as saying:

He was a prophet, powerful in word and deed before God and all the people. The chief priests and our rulers handed him over to be sentenced to death, and they crucified him; but we had hoped that he was the one who was going to redeem Israel (Lk 24:20-21).

The disciples had lost hope after Jesus' burial, believing him to be just another prophet. The only explanation that can account for the sudden turnaround in the lives of the disciples, evidenced by their subsequent public preaching and willingness to risk death, is the resurrection of Jesus. There is no evidence that the resurrection did not occur, and it is certainly possible for an omnipotent God to raise a person from the dead.

If Jesus did not rise from the dead, then there must be a reasonable explanation for the empty tomb. The only other explanation for the body of Jesus being missing from the tomb is that his followers, simple fishermen, overpowered the Roman guards at the tomb, stole the body, successfully hid the body from the Roman army and Jewish leaders, then risked their lives in order to promulgate a gigantic lie while at the same time preaching and living according to the highest of moral standards which included telling the truth. Deranged individuals and pathological liars do not behave in this way. The simplest and most logical explanation is that God sent the world a prophet whom he raised from the dead.

Jesus had appointed 12 of his followers to be apostles, and later he selected 72 others to go ahead of him into neighboring villages to heal the sick and announce the coming of the kingdom of God. After his ascension to heaven, these followers began teaching the gospel message of Jesus and making disciples, who later came to be called Christians. The Jewish Christians in Jerusalem sold their possessions and gave the proceeds to the needy. They met daily in the temple courts and discussed the teachings of the apostles. They continued to keep the laws of Moses including the offering of sacrifices in the temple. The church in Jerusalem was essentially a Jewish sect that believed the Son of God had come and died for their sins. For many years these Jewish Christians did not believe that Gentiles had access to God's redemptive plan without first becoming Jewish converts. The term "Christian(s)" itself only appears three times in the New Testament. Luke implies that the term was assigned to Jesus' followers by the non-believers in Antioch: "The disciples were called Christians first at Antioch" (Ac 11: 26). His followers called each other believers or disciples.

The Christian evangelist to the Gentiles was a Jew by the name of Paul who belonged to a Jewish sect known as the Pharisees and who once persecuted the Christians. Paul believed he had a vision in which he talked to Jesus, after which he began preaching the Christian gospel. Paul traveled throughout Asia Minor preaching the gospel in every town he passed through. Most of his converts were Gentiles, and Paul did not require them to follow the Jewish laws as the Christian Jews in Jerusalem continued to do. Some of these Jerusalem Christians were Pharisees who insisted that the Gentile Christians obey the laws of Moses. Even Paul had sacrifices offered in his behalf when he was in Jerusalem.

A council was held in Jerusalem where it was decided that the religion of Jesus was one of purification of the heart as opposed to being a ritualistic religion, and that the Gentile Christians need only abstain from eating food polluted by idols, meat from strangled animals, and blood, and abstain from sexual immorality. By having the Gentile Christians practice these few restrictions, they would not offend the Christians of the Jewish sect. From the very beginning of the Christian church, then, there were different sects based upon differing religious practices and beliefs. The council in Jerusalem was able to reconcile the two Christian sects by working out a compromise, but by AD 70 the Jewish sect was gone, with most of its members having perished in the Jewish war with Rome. A few survivors continued to meet as a small sect known as the Ebionites, and they were eventually declared to be heretical by the Gentile sect that had become the universal church. Within a couple hundred years a spirit of intolerance and legalism had infiltrated the church to the point that the "orthodox" church began persecuting and killing the Christians of the minority sects, usually over minor theological details.

For the first twenty years of its existence the Christian church used the Old Testament as its Bible along with the oral, unwritten teachings of Jesus. Paul founded many local churches that relied upon the memory of Paul's teachings that they received while Paul was in their midst. Eventually Paul began to write letters to these churches for their edification and instruction. These letters would be saved and passed around to other nearby churches. This was Paul's intent, as seen in his remark to the Colossians:

> After this letter has been read to you, see that it is also read in the church of the Laodiceans and that you in turn read the letter from Laodicea (Col 4:16).

No one knows what happened to Paul's letter from Laodicea; possibly it was lost or destroyed before anyone was able to make copies of it. In the 4th century a letter did appear entitled "Paul's Epistle to the Laodiceans." This letter survived to the 15th century where it was included in an English translation of the New Testament. A short time afterwards it was determined to be bogus.

In the second half of the first century biographies were written of the life of Jesus. Four of them were copied and circulated among the churches. These four biographies, which we call the four Gospels, are technically anonymous; the authors' names do not appear in the text of the books. In contrast, Paul introduces himself in the beginning of every one of his books; in fact, his name is the first word in all his letters. In spite of this, many scholars today believe that some of Paul's letters do not belong to the apostle Paul because the writing style and word usage is not that of Paul. Although the Gospels are anonymous, the names Matthew, Mark, Luke, and John are not seriously questioned as being the authors of the four Gospels. There were many Christian books in the first several centuries that used pseudo-names for the authors, usually the names of apostles, in order to add prestige to the books. Neither Mark nor Luke was an apostle, and Matthew was a tax collector, which would make him one of the less distinguished apostles. Consequently it is unlikely that the accepted gospel books used pseudo-names, and this adds credibility to the historicity of these books.

When the gospel records of the New Testament are subjected to the same historical tests as secular books of great age, they pass with flying colors. Names, dates, and places agree with those of archaeology and other first century historical sources. The writers of the New Testament books are generally unbiased as shown by the fact that they do not hesitate to record the faults of the apostles. The fact that the books of the Bible are historically reliable does not mean that they are without error. All books that pass the tests of historicity contain small errors, but the major events in those books can be relied upon as having happened. Concerning eyewitnesses to Jesus' resurrection, Paul had this to say:

> For what I received I passed on to you as of first importance: that Christ died for our sins according to the Scriptures, that he was buried, that he was raised on the third day according to the Scriptures, and that he appeared to Peter, and then to the Twelve. After that, he appeared to more than five hundred of the brothers at the same time, most of whom are still living, though some have fallen asleep. Then he appeared to James, then to all the apostles, and last of all he appeared to me also, as to one abnormally born (1Co 15:3-8).

Paul wrote this letter to the Corinthians in the 50's, about 20 years after the resurrection. He states that he received information from eyewitnesses to the resurrection, probably from the apostles living in Jerusalem. Those eyewitnesses include 500 followers who saw Jesus simultaneously after his death, most of whom were still alive at the time of Paul's writing.

The Corinthians could have checked with these eyewitnesses to validate Paul's claims concerning the resurrection of Jesus. If they could not find these eyewitnesses the Corinthians would undoubtedly have thrown Paul's letter in the garbage, in which case we would not be reading his letter today.

One historical event recorded in the New Testament that has had its historicity repeatedly questioned is the public census mentioned in Luke chapter two. While Quirinius was governing Syria during the reign of Herod the Great, Caesar issued a decree for a census to be taken, and Joseph and Mary were required to register in their hometown of Bethlehem. It may seem absurd that, according to Luke, citizens had to return to their hometown to register. However, it must have been common in that era because an official governmental order from the Prefect of Egypt dated AD 104 states that anyone residing outside of their province must return to their own homes for the regular census. Another objection to the census in Luke's Gospel is that, according to secular history, Quirinius began governing in AD 6, which is ten years after the death of Herod the Great; therefore Quirinius could not have governed during the reign of Herod as Luke reports. A coin, though, discovered by the archaeologist Jerry Vardaman, has Quirinius' name on it and places him as proconsul of Syria during the period 11 BC until after Herod's death, which confirms Luke's record of the census. Many people had the same Roman name, so there were evidently two men named Quirinius who ruled at two different times.

Skeptics have long asserted that the town of Nazareth did not exist at the time of Jesus' childhood. This town is not mentioned by the Old Testament, Paul, the Talmud, or any ancient historians. Archaeologists, though, have found a list in Aramaic describing the relocation of 24 priestly families from Jerusalem around AD 70, and one family had been moved to Nazareth. The population of Nazareth at that time has been estimated to have been no more than 480, so it is no wonder that such a small and insignificant town never appeared in any historical records outside of the New Testament.

There are more copies of manuscripts, by far, for the New Testament than for any other book of antiquity. Papyri fragments of the New Testament date back to the 2nd century, a mere 100 years after the autographs were written. There are 306 uncial manuscripts, which are written in all-capital Greek letters. Two of them date back to the mid-4th century. Minuscule manuscripts of the Greek New Testament, written in a cursive style, are about 2,856 in number. Lectionaries contain New Testament Scripture that was to be read at appointed times during the year. There are 2,403 lectionaries that have been catalogued. Besides the Greek manuscripts, there are ancient manuscripts of the New Testament in other languages. The Latin Vulgate manuscripts total to over 8,000, and there is a sum total of 8,000 manuscripts in Ethiopic, Slavic, and Armenian.

Next to the New Testament, the greatest number of Greek manuscripts belongs to Homer's *Iliad*, of which there are about 650. The *Iliad* was written around 800 BC, and the oldest copy we have dates to about 1,000 years later. Both the number of New Testament manuscripts and the age of the oldest ones in relation to the time the autographs were written attest to their historical accuracy.

The historicity of a first century Jesus is attested to by several secular historians of that era. Josephus, who wrote in the last decade of the first century, recorded the death of James, "the brother of Jesus who was called the Christ." In AD 115 the historian Tacitus recorded that Nero persecuted the Christians as a way to divert suspicion away from himself for the fire that burned Rome in AD 64. Finally, Pliny the Younger, a friend of Emperor Trajan, wrote to him around AD 111 asking for advice as to what to do with the Christians who "chant verses alternately amongst themselves in honor of Christ."

The major historical event in the New Testament books is that of the resurrection of Jesus, and so that event should be accepted as fact based upon the general historical reliability of the New Testament books. Historians have common sense rules to determine which historical documents are reliable and which are not, although there are present-day deconstructionists who declare all history books (at least the ones not written by them) to be fiction. The historical reliability of the New Testament is a stark contrast to that of the Book of Mormon. Archaeology has not substantiated any of its claims about events that supposedly occurred ages ago in North America. No remains of a Mormon city have ever been found, and no artifact or inscription has ever been found to verify even one Mormon person, place, nation, or name.

The teachings of Jesus should be accepted as being from God because Jesus claimed that they were and his claim is substantiated by his resurrection. Moreover, the possibility that Jesus' teachings came from the mind of man is remote; his principles of complete selflessness and pacifism are completely foreign to human nature. There are some Buddhists who teach these same principles, and there is no reason to deny that Buddhism may have received some of its teachings from God's inspiration. We should accept the teachings of Jesus as found in the New Testament books as being historically accurate because his teachings represent a large portion of these books which have been determined to be historically reliable. The teachings of Jesus therefore contain the truths of God, and this is the case regardless of whether or not the New Testament books are inspired of God, a subject that will be discussed shortly.

The Canon

In order to determine whether or not God had a hand in the formation of the New Testament we first must look back in history to see exactly how and when the books of the New Testament were written and when they were compiled. The 27 books of the New Testament were written between AD 50 and AD 100. The Christian church existed for at least 20 years before the first New Testament book was written. While the Jewish Christian church in Jerusalem continued to study and abide by the Old Testament and the oral teachings of the apostles, the Gentile churches that were begun by Paul initially had no writings or a permanent resident apostle as a source of authority. While Paul was staying with a church the leaders of that church could ask questions directly to Paul, but once he left town the church leaders had to rely on their memory concerning what Paul had told them about Jesus and how they were to conduct themselves as Christians.

Eventually Paul wrote to the churches he founded, but in the beginning Christianity was a religion founded upon the historic teachings, the death and resurrection of Jesus, and upon the oral transmission of those historical details. God did not give Christians a list of commandments engraved in stone, nor did he dictate a complete list of commandments to an apostle. These things God did with Moses and the Israelites at the time he made his covenant with them, and so the Jewish religion can be said to be founded upon the Ten Commandments and the Covenant commandments in the Torah. Christianity could not have been founded upon the New Testament since those books were not written until many decades later.

Some of these books were written by the apostles Matthew, John, Peter, and Paul. The other books, with the exception of Hebrews, were written by Mark, Luke, James, and Jude who were not apostles. The author of the book of Hebrews is unknown, although many Christians believe it was written by Paul. The writing style of Hebrews is not that of Paul's, and the letter does not begin with Paul's name as does his 13 epistles.

The 27 books of the New Testament were selected from a larger body of Christian books and were assigned to a category of books commonly called the "canon" by church officials during the 4th century. This word "canon" comes from the Greek word *kanon* meaning "rod," which was frequently used as a rule that was marked off in units of measure. Eventually this Greek word came to refer to the series of marks on the rod. It is in this sense that the word "canon" first came to refer to a series or list of the books that are included in the New Testament. Later, the "canon" also came to mean the "rule," or standard, for religious beliefs. The canonical books were initially selected to represent the authoritative teachings of the church; the idea of biblical inspiration was not in the beginning a prime consideration. The phrases "Old Testament" and "New Testament" first came into usage around the end of the 2nd century.

The selection of the New Testament books was based primarily on whether or not the author was an apostle or a close companion of one, how the teachings of each book compared to the accepted church doctrine of that time, and whether or not the book was written in the first century. Before the canon of the New Testament was closed in the 4th century there were smaller diverse collections of New Testament books being circulated in different parts of the world. Historical records indicate that the four Gospels and the writings of Paul were universally accepted from the beginning for teaching church doctrine and for reciting in church services.

A few of the New Testament books were not accepted by many churches during the first three centuries. The book of Revelation was not universally accepted until after the 4th century due to its mystical character. Two books that were ultimately rejected, the Letter of Barnabas and the Shepherd of Hermas, were considered to be Scripture by many churches during the first three centuries, as evidenced by their inclusion in the oldest extant Greek Bible called the *Siniaticus*. This Bible dates back to the 4th century and includes 29 New Testament books. Early church leaders such as Clement of Alexandria, Origen, Eusebius, and Athanasius quoted from the Shepherd of Hermas and ranked it among the sacred writings. Clement said it was "divinely expressed," and Origin called it "divinely inspired." Irenæus designated the book as "The Scripture."

The earliest historical list of New Testament books is known as the Muratorian Fragment, which was written at the end of the 2nd century and most likely represents the authoritative canon of the New Testament in Rome at that time. This list includes 21 of our 27 books, and leaves out Hebrews, James, 1st and 2nd Peter, and 2nd and 3rd John. Also included in this canon is the Apocalypse of Peter and the Wisdom of Solomon, the latter being included today in the Old Testament Apocrypha.

The Apocalypse of Peter is a book written by someone using Peter as a pseudo-name; hence it is included today in a body of works called the pseudepigrapha, so named because the authors used pseudo-names rather than their own. This collection of books includes the following:

- Gospel of Peter
- Gospel of Thomas
- Gospel of Matthias
- Acts of Paul
- Acts of Peter
- Acts of Andrew
- Acts of John
- Acts of Thomas
- Book of Enoch

Eusebius was bishop of Caesarea in Palestine in the first half of the 4th century. He is perhaps best known for his *Ecclesiastical History*, which would make him the second Christian historian after Luke. In his writings Eusebius divided the Christian books of that day into three categories: universally acknowledged, disputed, and spurious. The first category includes 22 of our 27 canonical books. The other five of our canonical books make up the "disputed" category: James, Jude, 2nd Peter, and 2nd and 3rd John. Among the "spurious" books are the Acts of Paul, the Shepherd of Hermas, the Apocalypse of Peter, the Epistle of Barnabas, the Teachings of the Apostles, and the Gospel According to the Hebrews. The Apocalypse of John (book of Revelation) was included in both the first and third categories, perhaps to reflect the animosity that some churches had towards the book. The Council of Laodicea in AD 363 rejected John's Apocalypse, as did Cyril, bishop of Jerusalem, and Gregory of Nazianzus who both produced lists of accepted Christian books in the latter part of the 4th century. The Christian scholar Jerome wrote in AD 414 that the Latin churches did not accept the book of Hebrews and that the Greek churches did not accept the Apocalypse of John.

It is believed that Eusebius was a religious advisor for Emperor Constantine, who asked him to prepare 50 copies of the Bible for use in Constantine's new capital at Constaninople. Although it is not known for certain which books made up the New Testament in these 50 Bibles, the consensus of opinion is that Eusebius included his "universally acknowledged" and "disputed" books which together make up our 27 books. The production of these 50 Bibles around AD 330 for the Roman Emperor may have more than any other event permanently fixed the Christian canon. The first historical list that represents our present-day canon of 27 books comes from Athanasius, the bishop of Alexandria, who included the list in AD 367 in his annual pastoral letter to the other Christian bishops. The first church council to specifically limit the canon of the New Testament to our 27 books was probably the Council of Hippo in AD 393.

The Christian theologian Augustine who converted to Christianity in AD 386 included a list of books in his work *On Christian Living* which is equivalent to our New Testament canon. In this same work Augustine explains what the criteria should be for selecting books for the canon:

> Among the canonical Scriptures he [the interpreter of the sacred writings] will judge according to the following standard: to prefer those that are received by all the catholic churches to those which some do not receive. Again, among those that are not received by all, he will prefer such as are sanctioned by the greater number of churches and by those of greater authority to such as held by the smaller number and by those of less authority. If, however, he finds that some books are held by the greater number of churches, and others by the churches of greater authority (although this is not a very likely thing to happen), I think that in such a case the authority on the two sides is to be considered as equal.[8]

Augustine knew that the issue of canonicity had not yet been settled among all churches. According to Augustine the question of canonicity was to be settled by democratic means. There is an implication in Augustine's criteria of three levels of authority among the books of the canon. The most authoritative books are to be those books that are accepted by all churches. But, if there are some books that are not universally accepted but are accepted by a majority of the churches including a majority of the larger, important churches, they are also to be accepted. Finally, the least authoritative books are those that are accepted by a majority of the churches but a minority of the larger ones, and those that are accepted by a minority of the churches but a majority of the larger ones. Apparently Augustine did not see a need for trying to establish divine inspiration for each book.

The Book of Enoch

Jerome remarked that the book of Jude was not accepted by many churches of his day because Jude "quotes from the apocryphal Book of Enoch." For Jerome the word "apocryphal" meant Christian writings that were suitable for reading for edification but not for establishing church doctrine. Here is the passage from Jude:

> Enoch, the seventh from Adam, prophesied about these men: "See, the Lord is coming with thousands upon thousands of his holy ones to judge everyone, and to convict all the ungodly of all the ungodly acts they have done in the ungodly way, and of all the harsh words ungodly sinners have spoken against him" (Jude 1:14-15).

In this passage Jude quotes a prophecy from the Book of Enoch that he believes was written by Enoch who was a direct descendant of Adam and was the father of Methuselah.

According to the books of Genesis and Hebrews, Enoch was taken by God directly to heaven and thereby escaped death; perhaps this is why Jude and others elevated him to the status of a prophet. Evidently Jude attributes to Enoch, who probably lived around 3000 BC, the writing of the Book of Enoch, which is estimated by scholars to have been written around 200 BC. Enoch lived about 2,800 years before the book was written, so it is doubtful that he is the author of the Book of Enoch. As a result, this book is included in the pseudepigrapha. Here is the passage directly from the Book of Enoch that Jude quoted from:

> And behold! He cometh with ten thousands of His holy ones
> To execute judgment upon all,
> And to destroy all the ungodly:
> And to convict all flesh
> Of all the works of their ungodliness which they have ungodly committed,
> And of all the hard things which ungodly sinners have spoken against Him (1 Enoch 1:9).

The Book of Enoch describes in detail how 200 angels (Enoch identifies the leaders personally by name) came down to earth before the days of Noah to mate with the women of our world, producing giant offspring, after which these angels were thrown into darkness until the Day of Judgment. The Pentateuch makes two brief references to this story:

> The Nephilim were on the earth in those days—and also afterward—when the sons of God went to the daughters of men and had children by them. They were the heroes of old, men of renown (Ge 6:4).
> And they spread among the Israelites a bad report about the land they had explored. They said, "The land we explored devours those living in it. All the people we saw there are of great size. We saw the

Nephilim there (the descendants of Anak come from the Nephilim). We seemed like grasshoppers in our own eyes, and we looked the same to them" (Nu 13: 32-33).

Jude and his fellow Jewish Christians were obviously familiar with the Book of Enoch because of his comment in verse five of his book that "though you already know all this, I want to remind you." Jude then proceeded to mention three events, two of them from the Old Testament. The middle event was from the Book of Enoch concerning the fate of the 200 angels:

> And the angels who did not keep their positions of authority but abandoned their own home—these he has kept in darkness, bound with everlasting chains for judgment on the great Day (Jude 1:6).

Jude mentions this event from the Book of Enoch along with the two events from the Old Testament, so he evidently considered this book to be just as authoritative as the Old Testament. The fate of the angels that Jude refers to in verse six is not found in the Old Testament, but Peter was also familiar with it:

> For if God spared not the angels when they sinned, but cast them down into hell, and committed them to pits of darkness, to be reserved unto judgment (2Pe 2: 4).

Jude and Peter used the Book of Enoch as their source for this story rather than the Bible, calling the heavenly beings "angels" rather than "sons of God" as the book of Genesis does and relating how God had cast them into darkness until the Day of Judgment instead of praising them as heroes as we find in the book of Genesis.

The Ethiopic Church, one of the oldest Christian

churches in the world, includes the Book of Enoch in its Bible. A remnant of this book was discovered in the 18th century in Qumran where the Dead Sea Scrolls were later found. The early Christian theologians quoted regularly from it, and one of them, Tertullian, considered it to be Scripture because Jude quoted from it and Peter referred to it in his second epistle. With credentials such as this, not to mention that Jude considered the author of the Book of Enoch to be a prophet, it is a wonder that the book of Jude, written by someone who was neither a prophet nor an apostle, was selected by the 4th century church to be in the canon and not the Book of Enoch.

There is no internal evidence in the New Testament to support the view that God personally selected these and only these books to be in the New Testament. *Neither Jesus nor the apostles made mention of a collection of 27 books that would be written in the future and be ordained by God as his Word.* Rather, the historical record shows that these 27 books were gradually selected over a period of several centuries from a larger group of writings by historical processes that are common in the forming of all religious traditions. There are many thousands of helpful, orthodox religious books written in the 20th century that can be found in the public library and bookstores. No one would consider picking out the best ones and compiling them into one volume to be called the "Word of God." Yet this is what happened in the 4th century.

Inspiration

Jesus referred to the Old Testament as the "Law and the Prophets" and as the "Scriptures" several times during his ministry, and Paul mentions "Scriptures" five times in his New Testament letters. It is evident that Jesus and the apostles considered the Jewish holy books to be "Scriptures," but it is not clear as to exactly what they meant when they used the term "Scriptures." The New Testament writers wrote in the Greek language, and the Greek word that is translated "Scriptures" is a word that simply means "writings." Jesus and the apostles, then, looked at the Old Testament as the writings of the Jewish prophets. These writings contain the Law of Moses (the Pentateuch), which Orthodox Jews believe to be word-for-word inspired, and the historical books, prophetic books and wisdom books which Jews believe were inspired by God in some way but not necessarily word-for-word. The Greek word translated "inspired" means "God-breathed," which may simply mean that God had breathed the impulse to write a book into certain individuals which they did with their own writing styles and imperfect knowledge. There is only one passage in the Bible that mentions the "inspiration of Scripture:"

> And how from childhood you have been acquainted with the sacred writings, which are able to instruct you for salvation through faith in Christ Jesus. All Scripture is inspired by God and profitable for teaching, for reproof, for correction, and for training in righteousness, that the man of God may be complete, equipped for every good work (2Ti 3: 15-17, RSV).

This passage is usually used as the proof-text for the belief that all 66 books of the Bible are the "Word of God." But Paul does not say in this passage which books are included in "all Scripture." When the church was established in AD 33, there were no New Testament books. They had not yet been written. The first New Testament book was penned about 20 years later. The first Christians were Jews, and they continued to use the Hebrew Scriptures as their Bible. The "Scriptures" that Paul, in the above passage, said Timothy had known since childhood was the Old Testament. This is the Bible that Timothy grew up with. So when Paul wrote, "All Scripture is inspired by God" he was referring to the Old Testament.

Of course, if Paul knew that there would be new Scriptures that would be written in the future, then he could have been referring to these new books as well. But Paul never mentioned the possibility of new books being written that would be deemed the "Word of God." He never claimed that his own letters were inspired, although he did believe that he received truths from God that he wrote about in his letters in his own words. Jesus never mentioned that there would be New Testament books written in the future. In fact, nowhere in the entire Bible is there mention of a group of 27 books that God wanted his authorship attached to. As far as Jesus and the apostles were concerned, the Law and the Prophets were the only holy Scriptures for the people of God. There is a reference to "other Scriptures" by the apostle Peter when he writes concerning Paul's letters:

> There are some things in them hard to understand, which the ignorant and unstable twist to their own destruction, as they do the other Scriptures (2Pe 3: 16 RSV).

In this passage Peter compared Paul's letters to the "other Scriptures," or other writings. Obviously Peter believed that Paul's letters contained spiritual truth, as he believed the Hebrew Scriptures did, but he did not claim that Paul's letters were inspired, and he made no mention of a group of 27 books that would later constitute a Christian Bible. Moreover, neither Peter nor Paul specified that inspired writings include the concept of word-for-word dictation by God. The Ten Commandments and the Book of the Covenant are the only writings that the Bible specifically implies are word-for-word inspired of God.

If the English word "Scriptures" in Paul's statement is replaced with the literal Greek translation, the result is "all writings are inspired by God." If this statement were true, then Paul would be saying that all writings, including secular ones, were inspired by God. A better translation is found in the ASV: "Every Scripture inspired by God is also profitable for teaching..." In other words, Paul is not talking about all "Scriptures," just those that are inspired by God. Most conservative and fundamental Christians interpret Paul's statement to mean that all 66 books of the Bible are inspired word-for-word and contain no error. It has already been determined that Paul was referring to the Old Testament when he used the phrase "every Scripture." Paul never implied that God dictated every word that he wrote in his letters. In the following passage Paul expressed his own opinion, which is indicative of the fact that Paul wrote about the truths of God in his own words:

> Now about virgins: I have no command from the Lord, but I give a judgment as one who by the Lord's mercy is trustworthy. Because of the present crisis, I think that it is good for you to remain as you are. Are you married? Do not seek a divorce. Are you unmarried? Do not look for a wife (1Co 7:25-27).

Here Paul gives his opinion, or "judgment," which he specifically states is not a command from God. Another indication that Paul wrote in his own words is the fact that he quoted from heathen sources several times in his letters. When Paul wrote to the Corinthians, "bad company corrupts good morals," he was quoting Meander (Thais, 218). In the book of Acts Luke records Paul quoting the Stoic poet Aratus (c. 270 BC), "We are his offspring." Paul also quotes Epimenides (a poet and prophet c. 600 BC) twice, once in Acts, "for in him we live and move and have our being," and once in Titus, "Cretans are always liars, evil brutes, lazy gluttons." Paul was a Hellenist Jew who grew up in the Greek world, so as a Greek scholar he would naturally be familiar with the written works of the ancient Greeks.

None of the New Testament writers claimed that the books they wrote were word-for-word inspired of God. In fact, they did not claim any kind of direct inspiration from God except perhaps when John said that he received a vision from God in his book of Revelation. If God did cause the New Testament authors to write exactly what he wanted, word-for-word, without the authors knowing it, then God would have infringed on the authors' freewill by compelling them to write his words.

Moses was not "inspired" to write the Book of the Covenant; instead he took dictation directly from God. Moses and God spoke to each other so that there was no need for inspiration. When God inspires someone to write, he gives them the urge, the impulse, and then it is the decision of the writer to fulfill that urge by writing a book using the writer's own words and writing style while making a few mistakes in the process. God may have inspired ordinary Christians such as Mark and Luke to write their Gospels, but he never claimed to have done so. The four Gospels are accepted as historically reliable books and valuable teaching aids partly because they substantially agree with each other. The Gospels and the other New Testament books do not need to be inspired of God in order for them to convey the teachings of Jesus to the world.

The belief that the entire Bible was word-for-word inspired by God is an example of a doctrine that is essentially supported by one Scripture verse that is easily misinterpreted and taken out of context: "all Scripture is inspired by God." Another example of a doctrine that is supported by one ambiguous verse is the belief that Peter was the first pope, the head of the church. This doctrine is based solely upon the statement by Jesus that "upon this rock I will build my church" and upon the supposition that "rock" refers to Peter. It is always a mistake to create a biblical doctrine from just one or two Scripture passages; this will be discussed later in the book.

Scholars have two explanations for why the New Testament should be accepted as the inspired "Word of God." One explanation is that the New Testament books were accepted as the "Word of God" by the first century local churches immediately upon reception. There is no evidence to support this hypothesis; in fact, historical evidence shows that before the 4th century many New Testament books were disputed and some non-canonical books were accepted by a large segment of Christendom as Scripture. Even if the first Christians who initially received the New Testament books did indeed consider them to be Scripture, there is no reason to accept their opinion. The first Christians in Jerusalem were wrong for insisting that the Gentile Christians obey the Law of Moses, and the first century churches would also be wrong if they insisted that Christian writings be elevated to the status of "Word of God." The other explanation is that the Holy Spirit led the New Testament authors in the writing of their books just as the Old Testament writers were led. The following passage is used to support this theory:

> But the Counselor, the Holy Spirit, whom the Father will send in my name, will teach you all things and will remind you of everything I have said to you (Jn 14: 26).

It is assumed that since the Holy Spirit inspired the writing of the Hebrew Bible for the Jews, it follows that the same would be done for the Christians. But Paul explicitly taught that the new covenant will not be a written one. According to the above passage, the Holy Spirit would teach the apostles and bring to their remembrance everything Jesus taught them. This is quite different from the belief that the Holy Spirit dictated every word that the apostles wrote in their letters. The apostles may have remembered everything taught them by Jesus and the Holy Spirit, but when they wrote their epistles the apostles used their own unique writing styles and inserted their own opinions as we have seen Paul do. Moreover, many of the New Testament books were written by ordinary Christians who were not apostles, and the author of Hebrews remains unknown, so there is no way of knowing if the Holy Spirit inspired those writers. Both explanations are theories that were created to support an ancient church tradition.

Another argument used to support the belief in the inspiration of the New Testament is that since the New Testament contains no contradictions it must be the "Word of God." It could not be the product of imperfect men. While the New Testament books are historically reliable and substantially agree on the teachings of Jesus, there are yet some discrepancies. Matthew records that Jesus went to the region of Gadarenes where he drove a legion of demons from one man and into a herd of pigs. According to Mark, Jesus went to the region of Gerasenes, not Gadarenes, and encountered two men who were possessed by demons, not just one.

A cursory examination of the following viewpoints of James and Paul reveals a contradiction in their teachings:

> The teaching of James:
> In the same way, faith by itself, if it is not accompanied by action, is dead...You foolish man, do you want evidence that faith without deeds is useless...You see that a person is justified by what he does and not by faith alone (Jas 2:17,20,24).
> The teaching of Paul:
> For we maintain that a man is justified by faith apart from observing the law...However, to the man who does not work but trusts God who justifies the wicked, his faith is credited as righteousness...For it is by grace you have been saved, through faith—and this not from yourselves, it is the gift of God-not by works, so that no one can boast (Ro 3:28, 4:5; Eph 2:8-9).

James believed that a person cannot be justified by faith without action and deeds. Paul believed that everyone is justified by faith apart from doing works and deeds. The trouble that Christians have in reconciling these two conflicting viewpoints is reflected in the fact that the doctrine of justification is one of the major causes of division between Catholics, Protestants, and other Christians. Because most Christians assume from the start that the whole Bible is the "Word of God," and then look for ways to prove this (a backwards process), they immediately assume that there are no contradictions in the Bible. This frequently puts them in the position where they are forced to formulate convoluted explanations for contradictions such as the one between James' viewpoint and Paul's viewpoint.

The New Testament books should be accepted just as they are purported to be by their authors. For example, the writer

Luke intended his two books (the Gospel of Luke, and the Acts of the Apostles) to be historical accounts, and nothing more. He wrote them for the benefit of someone named Theophilus, and no one else:

> Therefore, since I myself have carefully investigated everything from the beginning, it seemed good also to me to write an orderly account for you, most excellent Theophilus, so that you may know the certainty of the things you have been taught (Lk 1:3,4).

Luke never hinted at the possibility of his two books being considered the "Word of God." Luke never mentioned that his books should be read by anyone other than Theophilus, to whom he addressed both books. God himself never stated that Luke's books were inspired. Luke was a Christian historian, nothing more and nothing less. The same principle applies to all the New Testament books. The authors of the New Testament did not claim that their books were word-for-word the "Word of God," although they did believe that they were passing on God's instructions to the recipients of their books.

Some Christians believe that inspiration must be accepted on simple faith, but this is the same argument the Muslims use when they state that the Koran is the "Word of God." Only those books that history reveals were dictated by God to man with God's direct confirmation, such as the Book of the Covenant, can be reasonably called the "Word of God." God's authorship should not be arbitrarily assigned to any book even when religious tradition has done so for nearly two thousand years. Religious tradition was wrong with the geocentric theory of the solar system, and it is wrong with the biblical inspiration theory.

It is tempting to insist that it is a small step to elevate the Bible from that of an accurate, truthful historical record to the level of the "Word of God." This should not be done without having hard facts as evidence. To take any book of the Bible and arbitrarily say that it is God's Word would be paramount to putting words in God's mouth. Moreover, to make a false statement concerning the authorship of any book in the Bible could be considered libel. The four Gospels contain a record of God's message for mankind, the spoken words of Jesus. But it is something else entirely to claim that God is the author of every word in the Bible. It would be wise to first check to see whether or not God actually claimed to be the author of a particular book before stamping his signature on the cover.

God may have insured that the story of Jesus would be preserved for all time by giving Christians in the first century the impulse to write historical books about the life of Jesus. These books contain the normal errors that any historical document would include, but the simple teachings of Jesus are repeated so many times by so many different writers that the possibility of his message being garbled by the 4th century selection process, the copying process, or the translation process, is zero. The historical evidence shows that this is how the New Testament books have been preserved. The theory that God himself dictated these 27 books cannot be substantiated.

The New Covenant

The phrase "New Testament" can be misleading because it implies that the Christian Bible is the new official legal code given by God to mankind. This phrase was assigned by church officials to the collection of 27 Christian books that were compiled in the 4th century. It is derived from the phrase "new covenant" which appears only seven times in the Bible, once in the Old Testament and six times in the New Testament. Some Bible versions use "new testament" in place of "new covenant" in the text of the Bible, but they mean essentially the same thing. Because the author of the book of Hebrews makes comparisons between the old covenant (God's covenant with the Israelites) and the new covenant which was revealed at Jesus' crucifixion, many Christians believe that the new covenant is a written legal code that replaced the old written code. Paul, though, explained that while the old covenant was a written one, the new covenant was not:

> He has made us competent as ministers of a new covenant—not of the letter but of the Spirit; for the letter kills, but the Spirit gives life (2Co 3:6).

The new covenant is a spiritual one, not of the letter. Anyone who is judged according to a written law will always be found guilty of having transgressed it because no one can perfectly keep a written law; hence, as Paul says, "the letter kills." The new covenant is founded on a spiritual law, the law of faith, which Paul describes as "circumcision of the heart:"

> No, a man is a Jew if he is one inwardly; and circumcision is circumcision of the heart, by the Spirit, not by the written code...Where is boasting then? It is excluded. By what law? Of works? Nay, but by the law of faith...But now, by dying to what once bound us, we have been released from the law so that we serve in the new way of the Spirit, and not in the old way of the written code (Ro 2:29, 3:27 KJV and 7:6).

There can be no doubt that Paul contrasts the old covenant with the new by explaining that the one is a written legal code and the other is not. Since salvation and eternal life are linked to the spiritual condition of our heart rather than to a written legal code, this would explain why Jesus and the apostles never mentioned a Christian written legal code. The new covenant is nothing more than the promise of the forgiveness of sins for those who have repented of following their sinful nature, and have thus had their hearts circumcised:

> When you were dead in your sins and in the uncircumcision of your sinful nature, God made you alive with Christ. He forgave us all our sins, having canceled the written code, with its regulations, that

was against us and that stood opposed to us; he took it away, nailing it to the cross (Col 2:13).

The New Testament tells us about the new covenant, but unfortunately many Christians have assumed that the New Testament is identical with the new covenant. The compilation of the 27 books is deemed by many to be *the new covenant,* in spite of the fact that the Bible explicitly says that the new covenant is a spiritual covenant and not a written one. Even the Old Testament attested to a spiritual covenant when Jeremiah wrote concerning a new covenant, "I will put my law in their minds and write it on their hearts" (Jer 31:31).

Legalism

One of the primary causes of division in Christendom, legalism, is deeply rooted in religious culture. Many of the Pharisees, in their efforts to scrutinize and dissect every word of the Law of Moses and the oral law, practiced religious legalism. They were accused by Jesus of straining out a gnat and swallowing a camel, and of ignoring the most important matters of the law: faith, mercy, and justice. After the establishment of the church, many of the Jewish Christians in Jerusalem insisted that the Gentile converts abide by the Law of Moses. During the first council of the church as recorded in the book of Acts Peter stood up to announce that written law is a yoke that no one can keep perfectly:

> Now then, why do you try to test God by putting on the necks of the disciples a yoke that neither we nor our fathers have been able to bear? No! We believe it is through the grace of our Lord Jesus that we are saved, just as they are (Ac 15:10-11).

Partly because of the legal nature of the Law of Moses, Orthodox Jews consider the Torah to be word-for-word inspired by God. In any legal code the precise wording is very important to ensure that the laws are properly obeyed. The changing of just one word can alter the meaning of an ordinance. After Constantine made Christianity the official religion of the Roman Empire in the 4th century, the influence of Roman law hastened the institutionalizing of the Church and the formalizing of church laws and church dogma. From Judaism the Church borrowed the notion of the Sabbath day and feast days, incense and burning lamps, psalms, hymns, and choral music, vestments and prayers, priests, high priest (pope), and the institution of the synagogue (transformed into the Church). More importantly, the Church borrowed the notion of religious law from the Torah by elevating the Christian writings to the status of inspired law. All legal institutions need a written law, and the Church was no different.

This legalistic bent continues in Christianity to this very day. Just as the Israelites demanded of God that they be given a king to rule over them, many Christians today demand that God give them a written law to rule over them. Churches that believe that the New Testament is a written law spend enormous amounts of time analyzing every word in the New Testament to ensure that God's law is followed without mistake, and in the process they lose sight of the forest because they are so concerned with the trees. By treating the New Testament as a legal code of which every word was inspired by God, many churches have overlooked the intended meaning of the writers of the New Testament and as a consequence have developed Christian dogmas littered with false doctrines.

Christians who do not interpret the New Testament in the same way label each other as heretics because they believe that interpreting the New Testament differently is equivalent to breaking God's written law. In this way legalism divides Christendom by proclaiming the Christian books to be written law. In order to give the New Testament books the authority of written law, churches have had to elevate the Christian books to the status of divine authority. This was never the intention of Jesus and the apostles. Paul told Timothy that Scripture is:

Useful for teaching, rebuking, correcting and training in righteousness, so that the man of God may be thoroughly equipped for every good work (2Ti 3:16-17).

Paul does not tell Timothy that Scripture is a written law full of doctrines and dogma that must be believed and obeyed. Rather, Paul says that Scripture is to be used as a guide for training God's people to do good works. The only spiritual law that God has given to all people of every era, Jews and Gentiles alike, is the law of faith, a spiritual law which when put into practice becomes the law of love. This will be discussed in more detail shortly.

If God intended to give the world an error free book of commandments to serve as a legal code it would only be natural to believe that he would use a method similar to the one he used to transmit the Ten Commandments and the Book of the Covenant to the Israelites: direct dictation including instructions from God for periodic public recitation from the book and for the safekeeping of the book beside the Ark of the Covenant. God could have dictated his commandments directly to an apostle who would have written down God's words as he spoke. Afterwards God could have given instructions for the use and safekeeping of the book such as how frequently the book should be read in the churches, how copies and translations should be made, and where the book should be kept when not in use.

Since God made no mention of dictating any books other than the Book of the Covenant it is apparent that he expects mankind to be satisfied with the historical records of the teachings of Jesus and the apostles that have been handed down to us. These New Testament books are sufficiently accurate to teach the form of human behavior that God expects. However, they were never intended to be designated the "Word of God," or used as a legal code or a source of dogma.

It is a mistake to assume that because God gave the Israelites a legal code, which was primarily a civil code rather than a spiritual one, he will therefore bestow eternal life on individuals based upon the adherence to a legal code. Moreover, once this false assumption is made it becomes necessary to create a legal code, and the New Testament is usually chosen to be that code even though it is not written as a body of legal statutes. This legal code must then be deemed to be word-for-word inspired by God in order to give it the proper legal authority. The very fact that society is grounded firmly upon written laws influences many to believe that the spiritual realm must be governed the same way. The Bible does not mention a legal code that is to be used in determining the spiritual future of mankind; it expressly states otherwise.

Undoubtedly there are many people who would assert that Christianity and Judaism would be without a foundation and would fall apart without an infallible Bible, a written law. Indeed, there have been individuals in times past who, upon discovering that the belief in the Bible as the "Word of God" is based on tradition rather than fact, have rejected the historical facts of the Bible and the scientific evidence of a Creator. In other words, they threw the baby out with the bathwater and became atheists. The search for the demarcation line between truth and tradition should not be abandoned from fear of producing greater errors. Modern research in science, history, and archaeology continues to confirm, not deny, the existence of God and the historicity of the Bible.

God left mankind with three foundation stones on which to build faith. First, the complexity and beauty of his handiwork, the universe, are ample evidence that he exists. Second, the historical evidence of Jesus' miracles, teachings, death, burial, and resurrection is overwhelming and leaves us with the only conclusion that he was sent from God to show us the true meaning of righteous living. Finally, the personal experience of talking to God and having one's prayers answered solidifies one's faith in God's promises. Asking for God's guidance through prayer helps to facilitate the process of separating truth from religious traditions. The words of Jesus, which are printed in red in many Bibles, come very close to deserving the appellation "Word of God" since Jesus was sent from God to deliver those words to us, and those words have been accurately recorded in the Gospels.

Chapter Four

The English Bible

The first Bible used in the earliest English church was the Latin Bible, or Latin Vulgate, which was translated by Jerome between AD 383 and AD 405. This was the Bible of the Catholic Church for over a thousand years. It was King Alfred in the latter part of the 9th century who perhaps translated the first portion of the Bible into English: the Ten Commandments and extracts from Exodus that may have been from the Book of the Covenant.

The oldest English translation of the gospels is known as the *Wessex Gospels*. Here is the parable of the sower from Matthew 13:3-8 from this first millennium Old English Version:

Sothlice ut eode se sawere his saed to sawenne. And tha tha he seow, sumu hie feollon with weg, and fuglas comon and aeton tha. Sothlice sumu feollon on staenihte, thaer hit naefde micle eorthan, and hraedlice up sprungon, for thaem the hie naefdon thaere eorthan diepan; sothlice, up sprungenre sunnan, hie adrugodon and forscruncon, for thaem the hie naefdon wyrtruman. Sothlice sumu feollon on thornas, and tha thornas weoxon, and forthrysmdon tha. Sumu sothlice feollon on gode eorthan, and sealdon waestm, sum hundfealdne, sum siextigfealdne, sum thritigfealdne.[9]

While Old English bears absolutely no resemblance to modern English, Middle English can read with some difficulty. Some of the New Testament books were translated into Middle English towards the end of the 14th century. This text is from the Lord's Prayer in Matthew 6:9-13:

> Oure Fader that art in heuene, halewed be thi name. Thi kyngdom come to us. Thi wylle be don, as in heuene, and in erthe. Oure eche dayes breed yeue us to day. And foryeue us oure dettys, as we foryeue oure dettourys. And ne lede us not in temptacyon, but delyuere us of yuel. Amen.[10]

These early English translations were intended for clergy use only. The first English translation for lay people was produced by the Oxford theologian John Wycliffe. His first version appeared between 1380 and 1384. It was a literal, word-for-word translation of the Latin Vulgate that would have made for very awkward reading. All copies were done by hand; printing had not yet been invented. Later editions of the *Wycliffe Bible* introduced natural English word order and idiom. Early 15th century editions included the "Epistle of Paul to the Laodiceans." Later biblical scholarship concluded that this book was spurious. The General Prologue to the *Wycliffe Bible* defends the translation and circulation of the Bible in the vernacular tongue. The Latin Vulgate had been the only Bible used by Western Christendom for so long that tradition had transformed it into the one and only holy Bible; any other translation was considered to be a corruption of God's Word. The Latin Vulgate was even preferred over the Greek New Testament.

The *Wycliffe Bible* came to be seen as a product of the heretical sect of Lollards, and some of those instrumental in the production of this Bible were imprisoned or burned at the stake. A synod of clergy at Oxford, England, in 1408 forbade anyone to translate or even read a vernacular version of the Bible. This prohibition remained law until the Reformed religion was established in England.

One of the major events that put an end to the Middle Ages was the invention of the printing press. With the declining cost of paper and the development of an oily ink, the relatively low cost of printed books enabled the lower classes of society to educate themselves and thus to determine for themselves the difference between truth and church tradition. The invention of the printing press is credited to Johanne Gutenberg of Mainz. He printed a Latin Psalter in 1454, the oldest dated printed work, and several years later he printed the *Gutenberg Bible*. The Latin Bible was published about the same time, in 1456. The Pentateuch was printed in Hebrew in Italy in 1482, and the complete Hebrew Bible in 1488.

The first New Testament printed in Greek appeared in 1514. It was part of a six-volume set with the Latin Vulgate in parallel columns that was published years later by Cardinal Ximenes. Desiderius Erasmus, the Dutch humanist, was the first to print and publish the Greek New Testament, which he did in 1516. The editions of Erasmus' Greek New Testament were used by Martin Luther for his German translation (1522) and by William Tyndale for his English translation (1525). The capture of Constantinople by the Turks in 1453 prompted many Greek scholars to migrate to Western Europe along with their Greek manuscripts, which aided the study of the New Testament in Greek.

The man who published the first English translation of the New Testament, which became the basis for all English translations before the 20th century, is William Tyndale. Born in Gloucestershire in 1494, Tyndale received his Masters degree from Oxford in 1515. Early on Tyndale had the conviction that everyone should have direct access to the Bible in his or her own language. In discussion with one of his contemporaries, Tyndale said, "If God spare my life, ere many years I will cause a boy that driveth the plough shall know more of the Scripture than thou dost." These same sentiments were shared by Erasmus, who wrote in his preface to his Greek New Testament: "I wish that the farm worker might sing parts of them [the Scriptures] at the plough, that the weaver might hum them at the shuttle, and that the traveller might beguile the weariness of the way by reciting them."

After failing to gain permission to have the Bible printed in English in England, Tyndale sailed for Europe in 1524 and translated the New Testament from Greek into English while staying in Wittenberg and Hamburg. The city of Cologne refused to print his English New Testament, forcing Tyndale to acquire the services of a printer in Worms. It was here that the first English New Testament was printed, and shortly thereafter copies were sent back to England. The New Testament books are listed at the front of this Bible and appear as follows:

The bokes conteyned in the newe Testament

i. The gospell of saynct Mathew.
ii. The gospell of S. Marke
iii. The gospell of S. Luke.
iv. The gospell of S. Jhon.
v. The actes of the apostles written by S. Luke.
vi. The epistle of S. Paul to the Romans.
vii. The fyrst pistle of S. Paul to the Corrinthians.
viii. The fyrst second pistle of S. Paul to the Corrinthians.
ix. The pistle of s. Paul to the Galathians.
x. The pistle of S. Paul to the Ephesians.
xi. The pistle of S. Paul to the Philippians.
xii. The pistle of S. Paul to the Collossians.
xiii. The fyrst pistle of S. Paul vnto the Tessalonians.
xiv. The seconde pistle of S. Paul vnto the Tessalonians.
xv. The fyrst pistle of S. Paul to Timothe.
xvi. The seconde pistle of S. Paul to Timothe.
xvii. The pistle of S. Paul to Titus.
xviii. The pistle of S. Paul vnto Philemon.
xix. The fyrst pistle of S. Peter.
xx. The seconde pistle of S. Peter.

xxi.   The fyrst pistle of S. Jhon.
xxii. The second pistle of S. Jhon.
xxiii.The thryd pistle of S. Jhon.
    The pistle vnto the Ebrues.
    The pistle of S. James.
    The pistle of Jude.
    The revelacion of Jhon.[11]

Tyndale followed Martin Luther's format in his German New Testament, which set apart the books of Hebrews, James, Jude, and Revelation without numbering them. Luther did not believe that these four books had the same canonical quality as the other New Testament books. This belief is reminiscent of the doubts that many churches had in the first four centuries concerning the authority of these and other New Testament books. This is the Lord's Prayer as it appears in Tyndale's New Testament:

> O oure father, which art in heven halowed by thy name. Let thy kyngdom come. Thy wyll be fulfilled, as well in erth, as hit ys in heven. Geve vs this daye oure dayly breade. And forgeve vs oure treaspases, even as we forgeve them whych treaspas vs. Lede vs nott in to temptacion. But delyvre vs from yvell, Amen.[12]

Tyndale translated the New Testament from Erasmus' third edition of the Greek New Testament of 1522 into good English as opposed to a literal rendering of the Greek idiom. He used Luther's German New Testament as an aid, but generally remained closer to the Greek than did Luther.

In 1526 the Bishop of London, Cuthbert Tonstall, ordered all copies of Tyndale's New Testament within his diocese to be relinquished to him, whereupon he had them publicly burned at St. Paul's Cross. Later, when he was in Europe, the Bishop arranged to buy all the available copies of Tyndale's New Testament in order to take them back to London to be burned. Tyndale was elated at this turn of events because he was able to use the revenue to produce even more New Testaments and to revise his translation.

Tyndale completed his translation of the Pentateuch from Hebrew and had it published in 1530. His death prevented him from translating the entire Old Testament, although the translation of Joshua to 2 Chronicles that appears in *Matthew's Bible* is probably his. Tyndale lived out his final years on the Continent in the free city of Antwerp. The surrounding territory was part of the Holy Roman Empire that was ruled by the Emperor Charles V. In 1535 he was kidnapped and removed from Antwerp and taken to the fortress of Vilvorde where the Emperor had him strangled and burned at the stake in 1536. Tyndale's last words were "Lord, open the King of England's eyes." His prayer had already been answered, because an English version of the Bible based upon his work had begun to circulate in England a few months earlier with the permission of King Henry.

The first complete Bible to be translated, printed, and published in English is *Coverdale's Bible*. Myles Coverdale was a graduate of Cambridge, an Augustinian friar and an assistant of Tyndale. The Bible was printed in 1535 on the continent under the title *The Bible: that is, the holy Scripture of the Olde and New Testament, faithfully and truly translated out of Douche and Latyn into Englishe*. Despite this title, the New Testament is basically Tyndale's with some revisions using Luther's German (Douche) New Testament. The Old Testament was translated from German, and *Coverdale's Bible* was the first to separate the Apocrypha from the other Old Testament books as an appendix. The copies that were exported to England included a dedication to King Henry. *Coverdale's Bible* was evidently the answer to Tyndale's last prayer.

Matthew's Bible was printed in 1537 and included in the title these words: "truly and purely translated into English by Thomas Matthew." This Thomas Matthew was a pen name; the editor was a former associate of Tyndale by the name of John Rogers who was burned at the stake in 1555. The New Testament is Tyndale's, and the Old Testament consists of the books translated by Tyndale with the remaining books being Coverdale's. Both this version and the second edition of *Coverdale's Bible* was printed with the statement "Set forth with the kinges most gracious licence." In the year after Tyndale's death, then, two English Bibles were in circulation in England with the King's permission.

By 1538 many English bishops were encouraging their clergy to use the English translations, and the king issued an injunction requiring an English Bible to be installed in every church throughout the country. Because the notes in these English translations had a strong Protestant bent, it was suggested by Thomas Cromwell that a revision be made which would be more acceptable to the conservative clergy. The revision was assigned to Coverdale, and the following year the *Great Bible* was published. The name "Great Bible" is probably due to its size; every church was to have one permanently placed in a convenient location for use by the parishioners. This Bible was Coverdale's revision of John Rogers' revision (*Matthew's Bible*) of Tyndale's Bible.

The Reforming movement met with a setback in 1543 when Parliament passed an act "for the advancement of true religion and for the abolishment of the contrary." The act banned "the crafty, false and untrue translation of Tyndale" which revealed the ignorance of England's legislators concerning the fact that the accepted English Bibles were almost wholly based on Tyndale's work. It was made a crime for any unlicensed person to read or expound the Bible in public and for anyone belonging to the lower classes of society to even read the Bible in private. The religious climate in England grew worse in 1553 with the accession of Mary to the throne. Some men involved with Bible translation were executed, including John Rogers and Thomas Cranmer; others escaped to Europe. There were no attacks made, however, on the *Great Bible*.

In Europe the English exiles, under the leadership of William Whittingham, produced a translation in Geneva that was substantially Matthew's edition of Tyndale with changes included from the *Great Bible*. This version, called the *Geneva*

Bible, was published in 1560. The New Testament was based upon Tyndale's latest version, and the Old Testament books that had not been translated by Tyndale were translated for the first time directly from the Hebrew. The notes in the *Geneva Bible* were Calvinistic in doctrine which may have contributed to the strengthening of British Puritanism during the fifty years that the *Geneva Bible* was the household Bible of English Protestants. Seventy editions were published, most of them in England.

The first Bible to be printed in Scotland, in 1579, was the *Geneva Bible*, and it was the first Bible to be appointed for reading in the churches in that country. The *Geneva Bible* remained popular even after the publication of the *King James Version*. In the "Translators to the Reader" in the *King James Version* the Scripture quotations are taken from the *Geneva Bible*. The outspoken Calvinism of the *Geneva Bible* was unacceptable to the church and state leaders in England, and so the bishops under Archbishop Matthew Parker published the *Bishops' Bible* in 1568. It was basically a revision of the *Great Bible*.

In 1582 Gregory Martin published his translation of the New Testament in English for Roman Catholics. The work was done at the English College in Rheims, hence it was known as the *Rheims New Testament*. Martin's translation of the Old Testament was published in 1609 and was called the *Douai Old Testament* since the English College had been moved back to Douai. Both Testaments were translated into English from the Latin Vulgate, and together the Bible has been frequently called the Douai Bible. A thorough revision was made of this version in 1749 by Bishop Richard Challoner, and in 1810 this version was authorized for use by Catholics in the United States.

Soon after coming to England from Scotland where he was known as King James IV, England's King James I summoned a conference of theologians and churchmen. Not much was accomplished at the conference except for a proposal for a new translation that was submitted by Dr. John Reynolds, President of Corpus Christi College. The proposal resulted in the following resolution:

That a translation be made of the whole Bible, as consonant as can be to the original Hebrew and Greek; and this to be set out and printed, without any marginal notes, and only to be used in all Churches of England in time of divine service.[13]

By stipulating that the translation not contain any doctrinal or "marginal" notes, the members of the conference insured that a Bible would be produced that would be acceptable to all English speaking readers. King James himself assumed a leading role in organizing the work. Forty-seven men, including most of the leading biblical scholars in England, made up the translation committee. *The Bishops' Bible* was the basis for the new translation, which is called the *Authorized Version* (AV) in England and the *King James Version* (KJV) in the United States. It was a church council that "authorized" the new version to supersede the *Bishops' Bible* for reading in church services. The KJV was first published in 1611 and included the Apocrypha as did nearly all the earlier versions; it was not until 1626 that an edition was published without it.

The preface to the KJV Bible, called "The Translators to the Reader," explains the necessity for yet another revision of the English Bible and includes the following:

Truly, good Christian Reader, we never thought from the beginning that we should need to make a new translation, nor yet to make of a bad one a good one...but to make a good one better, or out of many good ones one principal good one...[14]

Although the translators did succeed in making a better translation, many errors found their way through the publishing process. One misprint in the KJV has been perpetuated to this present day: Matthew 23:24 is still printed as "strain at a gnat" instead of "strain out a gnat." The first edition had Jesus saying "There is no man good, but one, that is God"; this was later corrected to read "There is none good but one, that is,

God." In a 1631 edition the printer left out "not" in the seventh commandment "Thou shalt not commit adultery." As a result, this edition came to be known as the "Wicked Bible." The "Vinegar Bible" was printed in 1717, so titled because the chapter heading for Luke 20 read "The Parable of the Vinegar" rather than "The Parable of the Vineyard." In 1795 the "Murderers' Bible" appeared in which Jesus says in Mark 7:27 "Let the children first be killed," the word "killed" being substituted for "filled." One might be led to believe that King James himself was somehow responsible for the printing error in Psalm 119:161 which read "Printers have persecuted me without a cause."

Over the next few centuries there were English translations made which incorporated the discoveries of older Greek manuscripts. One example is William Whiston's *Primitive New Testament*, published in 1745. Whiston was Sir Isaac Newton's successor at Cambridge and is famous for his translation of Josephus. His translation is based on the KJV with revisions made to take into account older Greek manuscripts that were later labeled the "Western Text." Another example is the *New Translation* by John Nelson Darby who also translated the Bible into German and French and the New Testament into Italian. Joseph Bryant Rotherham's *The Emphasized Bible* is the first version to translate the name of God in the Old Testament, the tetragrammaton "YHWH," as Yahweh. Two translations of the Greek Septuagint Old Testament appeared in the 19th century, along with two Jewish translations of the Hebrew Bible: *The Twenty-Four Books of the Holy Scriptures* translated by Isaac Leeser and the *Jewish School and Family Bible* by A. Benisch.

The first major revision of the KJV began in 1870 with the following submission to the Upper House of Convocation of the Province of Canterbury:

> That a Committee of both Houses be appointed, with power to confer with any Committee that may be appointed by the Convocation of the Northern Province, to report upon the desirableness of a revision of the Authorized Version of the New Testament,

whether by marginal notes or otherwise, in all those passages where plain and clear errors, whether in the Hebrew or Greek text originally adopted by the translators, or in the translation made from the same, shall, on due investigation, be found to exist.[15]

The resulting translation, the *Revised Version* (RV), was published in 1885. Its American counterpart, the *American Standard Version* (ASV), first appeared in 1901. Many of the changes made from the KJV were due to the underlying Greek text from which the translation was made. The first printed Greek New Testament, published by Erasmus, and subsequent editions by others were based upon a few relatively recent Greek manuscripts that textual critics identify as the "Byzantine" text type. A 1633 edition contains the Latin preface "the text which is now received by all," and it is this advertising statement made by the printer which has resulted in the designation "Received Text," or *Textus Receptus*, which is substantially the same as the Byzantine text. All of the English Bible versions up to and including the KJV are based on the Received Text.

Scholars in the field of biblical textual criticism have to contend with over five thousand pieces of Greek manuscripts plus thousands of early translation versions as they seek to piece together a Greek New Testament that represents most closely the autographs. The consensus of the vast majority of scholars is that, generally speaking, the older the Greek manuscript the more it will agree with the autograph. Most Bible manuscripts of great age do not survive the ravages of time; hence as we go back in time we find fewer and fewer extant Greek manuscripts. The oldest Greek manuscripts are representative of the Western and Alexandrian text types, of which there are but a few. There are thousands of Byzantine text type manuscripts.

A few scholars believe that the more numerous the text type, the more likely that it represents the original writings of the New Testament authors. They also believe that the oldest manuscripts have survived only because they were never used

due to the errors they contained. In reality, the reason for there
being so many Byzantine manuscripts is the simple fact that in
the Empire of Byzantium the Greek language continued to be
read and spoken, so naturally all the Bibles in the East would be
in the Greek language. The number of Byzantine manuscripts
has nothing to do with their purity. In the West it was the Latin
Bible that was used by the church rather than the Greek Bible.
As a result there were few copies made of the Greek Bible in
the Roman Catholic Church after the 4th century, but there
are thousands of surviving Latin Bibles. As for why the oldest
manuscripts survived, it should be remembered that from
early on the church ferociously persecuted heretics, burning
them and their books. Therefore it can safely be assumed
that any Bible that was deemed to be full of errors would have
been committed to the flames. The oldest Bible manuscripts
survived because they were considered to be pure, and they
were found in very dry regions of the Middle East which helped
to preserve them.

Some of the most distinguished textual critics in England
worked on the RV. Two professors from Cambridge, B.F.
Wescott and F.J.A. Hort, believed that the two oldest Greek
manuscripts of that day, the Sinaitic and Vatican codices,
deserved the most weight in constructing a new Greek New
Testament text. These two men published a new edition of
the Greek New Testament five days before the *Revised New
Testament* was published. Their devotion to the two great
codices is now seen as somewhat excessive but their Greek text
is still considered a major improvement on the Received Text.

The most scathing review of the RV came from the 19th
century contemporary Dr. John William Burgon. He did
not care for the translation work, which he said was "...an
unreadable Translation, in short; the result of a vast amount of
labour indeed, but of wondrous little skill..." What upset him
the most, though, was the underlying Greek text, about which
he says,

   is nothing else but a poisoning of the River of Life

at its sacred source. The Revisors, (with the best and purest intentions, no doubt,) stand convicted of having deliberately rejected the words of Inspiration in every page.[16]

Dr. Burgon did not like the fact that many passages in the KJV were determined to be later additions to the original text and so were relegated to the margin in the RV, such as the passage about the angel troubling the water of the pool of Bethesda (Jn 5:4) and the Ethiopian's confession of faith (Ac 8: 37). The last twelve verses of Mark are printed as an appendix to this Gospel. The textual evidence weighs in favor of this ending to Mark as being a later addition. Moreover, the statements supposedly made by Jesus in these last twelve verses are out of character for him; suddenly Jesus is preaching a dual salvation process of faith and baptism instead of his simple message of "he who believes in him will not perish," and his disciples are now snake handlers and imbibers of poison.

The most blatant addition is found in 1 John 5:7-8 where the KJV includes the passage of the three in heaven that bear witness. These words were not included in any original Greek text or the earliest editions of the Latin Vulgate. They are seen first in the writings of a Christian Spaniard named Priscillian who was put to death for heresy in AD 385. The passage shows up later in copies of the Latin Bible. Erasmus left these words out of his printed Greek text and challenged anyone to produce a Greek text that included this passage. A Greek manuscript only twenty years old was found to include the disputed words–but the manuscript was a translation of a Latin text. Dr. Burgon's lonely crusade for the Received Text was continued in the next century by Dr. E.F. Hills.

The translators of the RV leaned, perhaps too far, toward the Formal Equivalence translation method which meant that the almost word-for-word accuracy made the English text difficult to follow and awkward; hence the RV never replaced the KJV in public or private worship. The other major translation method is Dynamic Equivalence, which translates phrase for phrase or sentence for sentence so that the resulting English text reads more like natural English. Every Bible translation tries to find a balance somewhere between the two extremes of a Greek Interlinear and a paraphrase such as the *Living Bible*.

The Old Testament of the RV was more of a success. The translators used the Masoretic Text as did the KJV translators rather than creating a new text as they did with the Greek New Testament. The 19th century scholars understood the Hebrew text better than the 17th century scholars who translated the KJV, and as a result English readers could better understand the Old Testament. Further advances have been made in the 20th century in understanding Semitic languages that have resulted in the Old Testament, particularly the book of Job, being even easier to understand in our modern translations.

As the understanding of ancient biblical languages continues to improve and as the English language continues to change, the need for more accurate Bible translations in English continues to grow. The first translation after the ASV of 1901 is the *Twentieth Century New Testament* published in 1902 that was translated from Westcott and Hort's Greek text. One of the translators was Dr. Richard Francis Weymouth who published his own Greek text called the *Resultant Greek Testament*. Afterwards he produced his own English translation, the *New Testament in Modern Speech*, which was published in 1903. One noteworthy difference in his version was the translation of the Greek word *aion* into "ages" instead of the usual "eternal." Thus, "eternal life" becomes "the life of the ages," which is a definite improvement in the Greek translation although "the life of the age to come" would be more understandable. There will be more discussion later on this Greek word *aion* as it relates to eternal punishment.

In 1937 work was begun by the Council of Religious Education to revise the ASV. Its goal was to:

> Embody the best results of modern scholarship as
> to the meaning of the Scriptures, and express this

meaning in English diction, which is designed for use in public and private worship and preserves those qualities, which have given to the King James Version a supreme place in English literature.[17]

A committee of 32 scholars did the translation work, and the *Revised Standard Version* (RSV) was published in 1952. It is a revision of previous revisions stretching back in time past the KJV to Tyndale himself. The RSV used modern English as seen by the replacement of archaic words such as "saith," "sendeth," "thou," "thee," "thy," and "thine," and the replacement of the Semitic idiom "And it came to pass."

The translators used the Isaiah scroll, one of the Qumran texts from the Dead Sea Scrolls, to solve a mystery. Isaiah 21:8 is translated from the Masoretic Text as either "And he cried, A lion" or "And he cried as a lion," neither of which makes any sense in the context. The same verse in the Isaiah scroll translates as "Then he who saw cried," referring to the watchman in verse six who is waiting for the approach of a messenger. At some time in the distant past a Hebrew word had two letters transposed and this error was apparently copied into the Masoretic Text.

The RSV translates Isaiah 7:14 as "Behold, a young woman shall conceive" instead of "Behold, a virgin shall conceive" because the Hebrew word *almah* which appears in this verse means young woman; there is another Hebrew word for virgin. Matthew 1:23 is translated in the RSV as "Behold, a virgin shall conceive" because Matthew is quoting from the Greek Septuagint and not the Hebrew Old Testament. The Septuagint uses the Greek word *parthenos,* which means "virgin." Thus, the RSV does not attempt to force the Book of Isaiah in its Hebrew form to agree with Matthew's quotation of the same passage from the Septuagint.

In the British Isles a joint committee was established in 1946 that included the Church of England and the Church of Scotland. Its purpose was to prepare a new translation in modern English rather than simply revise the RV. The resulting *New English Bible* (NEB) was published in 1970. The guiding principles of the translation are explained by Dr. C.H. Dodd, the General Director:

> It is to be genuinely English in idiom, such as will not awaken a sense of strangeness or remoteness. Ideally, we aim at a "timeless" English, avoiding equally both archaisms and transient modernisms.[18]

At a later date Dr. Dodd pointed out in an article that a word-for-word translation from one language to another is impossible because a large number of words in any language will have no corresponding word with the same meaning in another language. The unit in translation must be the phrase or the sentence, not the word. The overruling principle should be intelligibility. It should be the translator's goal to produce in the reader a response similar to that which was evoked in the minds of those who read the original books. At the same time, translators should always realize that they practice an impossible art.

There was no single text type used as the underlying Greek text in the NEB as was the Alexandrian text type that was used by Westcott and Hort for the RV. The Introduction to the NEB states that,

> The present translators therefore could do no other than consider variant readings on their merits, and, having weighed the evidence for themselves, select for translation in each passage the reading which to the best of their judgment seemed most likely to represent what the author wrote.[19]

Here is a list of other English translations that have made their appearance in the 20th century:
- *The Holy Bible in Modern English*, by Ferrar Fenton, 1903
- *The Holy Scriptures according to the Masoretic Text*, by the Jewish Publication Society of America, 1917
- *A New Translation of the Bible*, by James Moffatt, 1923; in the

beginning of the Gospel of John, Moffatt chose to retain the Greek word in its transliterated form, "Logos," since any English translation of the Greek word is inadequate, including the usual translation "Word."

- *The Complete Bible: An American Translation*, by Edgar J. Goodspeed, 1927
- *The Bible in Basic English*, by S.H. Hooke, 1949; a simple form of the English language produced by C.K. Ogden for people whose native language is not English, Basic English was used by Dr. Hooke for this translation after he increased its vocabulary from 850 words to 1,000 words.
- *The Authentic New Testament*, by Hugh J. Schonfield, 1955; Dr. Schonfield is a distinguished Jewish scholar.
- *New Testament in Modern English*, by J.B. Phillips, 1958; This translation has sometimes been called a paraphrase, but it might be more accurate to say that it straddles the border between the two.
- *The Holy Bible: The Berkeley Version in Modern English*, by Gerrit Verkuyl, 1959
- *The Amplified Bible*, by the Lockman Foundation, 1965
- *The New World Translation*, by the Watchtower Bible and Tract Society, 1960; This is the Bible version used by Jehovah's Witnesses and is well known for its unusual translation of John 1:1, "The Word was a god."
- *The Jerusalem Bible*, 1966; This is the English counterpart of a Roman Catholic French translation. The three heavenly witnesses of 1 John 5:7 have been removed with the footnote: "not in any of the early Greek MSS, or any of the early translations, or in the best MSS of the Vulgate itself."
- *The Modern Language Bible*, 1969; a revision of the Berkeley Version.
- *The New American Bible*, by the Confraternity of Christian Doctrine, 1970; this is a Roman Catholic English version that was translated from the original languages.
- *The New American Standard Bible*, by the Lockman Foundation, 1971; a revision of the ASV of 1901, this

version uses "the LORD," as does the RSV, in place of "Jehovah" which was a medieval spelling based upon a misunderstanding of vowel points in the Hebrew text. A Formal Equivalence translation.

- *The Living Bible*, by Kenneth N. Taylor, 1971; a paraphrase that was originally intended for Dr. Taylor's children.
- *The Common Bible*, 1973; an ecumenical edition of the RSV.
- *Good News Bible*, by the American Bible Society, 1976
- *The New International Version*, the New York Bible Society, 1978; translated by evangelical scholars from many parts of the English-speaking world, this version is the best selling Bible in the United States. A Dynamic Equivalence translation.
- *The New King James Version*, 1982; a revision of the KJV for easier reading, this version is based on the Received Text. A Formal Equivalence translation.
- *The New Century Version*, 1986; translated specifically for children.
- *The Twenty-First Century King James Version*, 1994; the KJV is revised again to include modern spelling, paragraphing and capitalization.
- *The English Standard Version*, Good News Publisher, 2001; an international effort by over 100 scholars, this version uses the USB/Nestle-Aland Greek Text (27th edition). A Formal Equivalence translation.

Chapter Five

Interpreting the Bible

The Book of the Covenant was written in a precise legal fashion, judging from the commandments that are scattered throughout the Pentateuch. Our own legal statutes are written in an unambiguous legal manner (in most cases). Figurative language has no place in a legal code. As it is, most of the Bible is written in a literary fashion, not a legal fashion. Figures of speech abound. Since the Bible was written long ago by people of foreign cultures who wrote in foreign languages, it is not possible to determine the intended meaning of every passage in the Bible. One cannot read the minds of the Bible authors to determine in every instance when a figure of speech or idiom was being used. By using the principles of interpretation, biblical hermeneutics, it is possible to arrive at the proper understanding of most Bible passages. The rules of biblical hermeneutics include examining the immediate context such as the paragraph and book in which a particular passage is found, examining the historical and cultural context of that passage, determining whether that passage should be taken literally or figuratively, checking for translation errors, and allowing the major themes of the Bible to interpret that individual passage. One of the most frequent errors made by Christians is that of lifting a Bible passage out of its context and giving it a meaning that is different from the one intended by the writer in order to substantiate a particular doctrine.

If the passage in the book of Joshua where Joshua told the sun to stop in its path around the earth was interpreted literally, the reader would be forced to conclude that the sun revolves around the earth, which millions of Christians did for centuries. But it is a well-known scientific fact that the earth revolves around the sun, so there must be another explanation for what Joshua said. Either Joshua was familiar with modern facts of astronomy and was making an idiom when he implied that the sun revolved around the earth, or he truly believed as did most everyone else in his day that the earth was the center of the solar system. *If an interpretation of a Bible passage leads to a contradiction with a well- known fact or a biblical theme, then that interpretation must be assumed to be incorrect.*

One of the most important principles of biblical hermeneutics is that of using a large body of biblical passages worded in plain language to interpret or better understand the few biblical passages that appear to teach something different on the same subject. In other words, let the large body of Scripture interpret the smaller body. The few passages should never be used to interpret the many. To put it on a grander scale, the major themes of the Bible should be used to interpret the other subject matter in the Bible. One should never draw a conclusion from a Bible passage that contradicts a major theme of the Bible. For example, the Bible is awash with references to God's attributes of love, justice, and mercy. The words "justice" and "mercy" each appear over one hundred times in the Bible, and the word "love" appears over five hundred times. These attributes of God represent a major biblical theme. If a Bible verse appears to contradict this theme, such as Matthew 25:46 which mentions "eternal torment," then a different explanation must be sought–in this instance the word "eternal" is a mistranslation of the Greek word.

Chapter One discussed the philosophical basis for believing that God must have the attributes of love, justice, and mercy. This philosophical conclusion is confirmed by the Bible, which teaches that God is love. Also in Chapter One it was determined that it would be a contradiction for a God of love, justice, and mercy to eternally punish anyone. There is nothing just or merciful in punishing someone endlessly for a crime of limited duration. Some Christians may object, stating that God's standards of love, justice, and mercy are so different from ours that we cannot fully understand them. There are several reasons why this could not be true. First, the Bible says that man was made in his image. Therefore what man considers to be the very highest of moral standards will simply be the spiritual reflection of God's moral standards. Paul wrote to the Christians at Rome that God has instilled his moral standards in the conscience of the individual:

> Indeed, when Gentiles, who do not have the law, do by nature things required by the law, they are a law for themselves, even though they do not have the law, since they show that the requirements of the law are written on their hearts, their consciences also bearing witness, and their thoughts now accusing, now even defending them (Ro 2:14-15).

Since people have both a human nature and a spiritual nature it is sometimes easy to confuse the two. For example, the human attributes of revenge, anger, and hate can overshadow and even bury the spiritual attributes of love, fairness, and mercy. Revenge is frequently mistaken for justice. The Bible is a guide to help delineate between the two natures. Second, the Bible describes God's love and mercy as being boundless and endless. God's moral attributes are different from those of human beings only in terms of degree. John said, "God is love" and "God is light, in him there is no darkness at all." There is not even a hint of darkness in his character. Third, if God says that he is just and commands his created beings to be just, then God is implying that he is holding people to his standards of justice:

> Do not pervert justice; do not show partiality to the poor or favoritism to the great, but judge your neighbor fairly (Le 19:15).
> The LORD loves righteousness and justice; the earth is full of his unfailing love (Ps 33:5).

The Old Testament is full of examples demonstrating how judicial punishment should fit the crime, such as the injunction given to the Israelites to give a "life for a life, tooth for a tooth, hand for a hand...." Because God is infinitely more just than people are, he will not punish anyone to a greater extent than the crime deserves. Any crime of limited duration will be met by God with a punishment of limited duration.

God offers proof of his unbounded love. Common sense dictates that the greatest love one can have for another is demonstrated by giving one's life for another. Jesus confirmed this principle when he said, "Greater love has no one than this, that he lay down his life for his friends." The Christian philosopher Kierkegaard believed that the crucifixion of Jesus makes no rational sense and that one must simply accept this event on faith. In actuality, the death and resurrection of Jesus make perfect sense because God knew that it would prove beyond doubt his unlimited love for mankind. God's fairness towards his created people is without bounds, as are all his attributes. Paul told the Romans that:

> God "will give to each person according to what he has done." To those who by persistence in doing good seek glory, honor and immortality, he will give eternal life. But for those who are self-seeking and who reject the truth and follow evil, there will be wrath and anger. There will be trouble and distress for every human being who does evil: first for the Jew, then for the Gentile; but glory, honor and peace for everyone who does good: first for the Jew, then for the Gentile. For God does not show favoritism (Ro 2:6-11).

God does not play favorites where our eternal destiny is concerned. He loves all of his created children and he gives us all an equal opportunity to repent and live a righteous life. Until each individual repents, he or she will experience "wrath and anger" and "trouble and distress," because these are the natural outcomes of living a life of evil. Since God has unlimited patience, he will bear with each of his created children until they repent:

> But for that very reason I was shown mercy so that in me, the worst of sinners, Christ Jesus might display his unlimited patience as an example for those who would believe on him and receive eternal life (1Ti 1: 16).

The apostle Paul was the worst of sinners because he had Christians put to death for their beliefs. Yet God miraculously intervened in Paul's life when he was traveling to Damascus to put the Christians there in prison. God's mercy and patience is unlimited and he shows no favoritism. It does not matter what circumstances a person was born under, whether a person lived in a country where the name of Jesus was unknown, or whether a person was reared and indoctrinated in a religion other than Christian. God went the extra mile to help Paul, and he will put forth every effort until every one of his created children has repented, either in this life or in God's unrevealed plans for the future. God has all eternity to persuade his created children to repent, so there is no reason for him to limit his efforts to the brief moment of time available in this life. Paul implies that one day all will have repented and will have received eternal life:

> For if, by the trespass of the one man, death reigned through that one man, how much more will those who receive God's abundant provision of grace and of the gift of righteousness reign in life through the one man, Jesus Christ. Consequently, just as the result of one trespass was condemnation for all men, so also the result of one act of righteousness was justification that brings life for all men (Ro 5:17-18).

Paul explained that through Adam death comes to all men, but through Jesus justification and life is given to all men. To the Corinthian Christians he said, "For as in Adam all die, so in Christ all will be made alive." One would expect no less from a God of unlimited love and mercy. The punishment that evildoers receive, either in this life or in the next, is of limited duration because their crimes were committed within a limited span of time. A God of unlimited justice and mercy equitably matches punishment with the crime.

A common notion in Christian theology is the "paradox," an apparent contradiction that simply must be accepted even though it is not understood. Thus, Reformed theology can teach that a God of love, justice, and mercy arbitrarily assigns millions of people who have no free will to eternal torment by explaining it as a paradox. Not much better is the belief of most Christians that while everyone has a free will, those who have not heard the Gospel of Jesus in this life will suffer eternal punishment. There are many people who had heard the Gospel but rejected it because they had been indoctrinated in the religion of their parents and taught that the resurrection of Jesus was a myth, but this is no excuse according to orthodox Christians who consign these unbelievers to eternal punishment.

Those who believe (correctly so) that all children who die go straight to heaven are forced into a second contradiction if they believe in the first contradiction of eternal torment. Most orthodox Christians would agree that the majority of the children of the world who attain adulthood will die and be condemned to hell. Could there be a greater righteous act than that of guaranteeing that a person avoid eternal punishment? Abortion sends an unborn child straightway to heaven, whereas if that child had grown to adulthood the orthodox belief states that the adult would probably wind up eternally damned. A belief that leads to the conclusion that abortion could be considered a righteous act is a belief mired in contradictions.

The Doctrine of Hell

There are simple explanations for the few Bible passages that appear to teach eternal punishment or annihilation, ranging from the mistranslation of words from Greek to English to taking literally Bible phrases that are actually figures of speech. In the English language the word "hell" is defined as a place of eternal torment. However, there is no Hebrew or Greek word in the Bible that means "eternal torment." The Hebrew word *Sheol* occurs 66 times in the Old Testament and is translated "hell" in some translations, but *Sheol* simply means the place, or state, of the dead. An accurate translation of *Sheol* into English would be "the grave." In the Old Testament everyone who died went to *Sheol*, the grave, the righteous and the unrighteous. Also, the Old Testament rarely if ever discussed the subject of life after death. There is no evidence that the Israelites believed in punishment after death.

The Sadducees did not believe in heaven, hell, or the resurrection of the dead for the simple reason that those subjects were not taught in the Hebrew Bible. They only used the Old Testament for their beliefs and rejected the oral teachings of the Pharisees, who taught the existence of eternal punishment. When the Hebrew Old Testament was translated into Greek (the Septuagint), the Hebrew word *Sheol* was translated into the Greek word *Hades*, a word that also means "the grave." This Greek word appears in the New Testament eleven times and could be translated "grave" when taken literally or "destruction" when translated figuratively. It is a gross mistranslation to use the English word "hell" for the Hebrew word *Sheol* and the Greek word *Hades*.

Another Greek word that is translated "hell" in the New Testament (12 times) is *Gehenna*. This word is derived from the two Hebrew words *ge-Hinnom*, and is translated literally "valley of Hinnom." This valley was owned by a person named Hinnom and is located on the south side of Jerusalem. *Gehenna* is a physical place in Palestine and has an interesting, if somewhat morbid, history. In Jewish history some of the wicked kings and their subjects offered sacrifices to the god Molech in this valley. Sometimes they offered their children as burnt offerings. When the good king Josiah came to the throne this abominable practice was stopped and *Gehenna* was turned into Jerusalem's garbage dump. Fires were kept burning in *Gehenna* to keep the stench down, and worms helped decompose the animal carcasses in the dump. This place was used as an analogy by Jesus who took the temporal woes (not eternal) that accrue to the wicked and compared them to being tossed into Jerusalem's garbage dump:

> It is better for you to enter the kingdom of God with one eye than to have two eyes and be thrown into hell [*Gehenna*], where "their worm does not die, and the fire is not quenched" (Mk 9:47-48).

There is one other Greek word in the New Testament that is translated "hell," and that is *Tartarus*. This is a word from Greek mythology that denoted the place below the earth where gods imprisoned their enemies. *Tartarus* was originally a place located below Hades; later it was used to refer to the entire underworld. Peter used this word when he referred to an event described in the apocryphal Book of Enoch:

> For if God did not spare angels when they sinned, but sent them to hell [*Tartarus*], putting them into gloomy dungeons to be held for judgment (2Pe 2:4).

Sheol, Hades, Gehenna, and *Tartarus* are all specific places, either real or mythological, and as proper nouns these words should have been left unaltered in the translation process. These words should not have been translated "hell" any more than Sodom and Gomorrah should have been, and they never refer to a place of eternal punishment in the Bible. Even though Peter spoke of the mythological *Tartarus* where gods and angels were supposedly imprisoned, he specified that it was just a waiting place until judgment.

Most translations of the English Bible have a few references to everlasting punishment and eternal fire. The words "everlasting" and "eternal," though, are mistranslations of the Greek word *aionios* in these passages. The noun *aion* from which the adjective *aionios* is derived means "age." Strong's Concordance acknowledges that the literal meaning of *aion* is an "age" (*New Strong's*, 1984), as do many other scholars and commentators. *Vine's Dictionary of New Testament Words* states that the literal meaning of *aion* is "age" and that *aionios* is used in the New Testament to denote duration that is not endless. Dr. Marvin Vincent in his *Word Studies of the New Testament* goes even further and states that these words never in themselves denote "endless" or "everlasting." There is a Greek word *aidios* (very similar in spelling to *aionios*), which means eternal, and which is only used twice in the New Testament. Paul used it once in reference to God, "his eternal power," and Jude used it once, "bound with everlasting chains for judgment," when referring to the angels in the Book of Enoch who were committed to the mythological *Tartarus* to await judgment. If God's punishment of the wicked were indeed eternal, then Jesus and the apostles would have either used the Greek word *aidios* or one of several other words that mean "endless." The English word "eon" comes from the Greek word *aion*, and it means a long period of time, not forever.

The Jewish historian Josephus, who lived during the first century, wrote his epic books in Greek. Josephus knew which Greek word meant "age" and which meant "eternal." When alluding to the Pharisees' belief in eternal punishment he used the Greek words that mean eternal, *aidion* and *aidios*, and not *aion* or *aionios,* which mean age or ages:

> They believe...that wicked spirits are to be kept in an eternal imprisonment [*eirgmon aidion*]. The Pharisees say all souls are incorruptible, but while those of good men are removed into other bodies those of bad men are subject to eternal punishment [*aidios timoria*].[20]

The Pharisees regarded the penalty of sin as torment without end. They called it *eirgmon aidion* (eternal imprisonment) and *timoria adialeipton* (endless torment). Another Jewish sect called the Essenes, according to Josephus, also "allot to bad souls a dark, tempestuous place, full of never-ceasing torment [*timoria adialeipton*], where they suffer a deathless torment [*athanaton timorion*]."

In the Book of Enoch we find the statement "For they hope to live an *aionian* life, and that each one of them will live five hundred years." The phrase "*aionian* life" is the same Greek phrase that is translated in our New Testament as "eternal life," and here in the Book of Enoch it represents a life of only 500 years. In the early Roman Empire periodic games were held and were referred to as "secular" games. Herodian, who wrote in Greek about the end of the 2nd century AD called these *aionios* games. Obviously those periodic games could not have been eternal. Josephus used the word *aionos* with its meaning of limited duration and applied it to the imprisonment of John the Tyrant, to Herod's reputation, to the glory acquired by soldiers, and to the fame of an army as a "happy life and '*aionian*' glory." He used the word as the New Testament does to denote limited duration, but when he described endless duration he used different terms.

When describing the doctrine of the Pharisees, *aidion* and *athanaton* are Josephus' favorite terms for endless duration, and *timoria* (torment) for punishment. The Pharisees' oral tradition taught eternal punishment, and they were rebuked by Jesus on several occasions for "setting aside the commands of God in order to observe your own traditions." Since the idea of eternal punishment did not come from the Old Testament the Pharisees may have borrowed it from pagan mythology and incorporated it into their oral traditions.

Jesus referred to the punishment of sin as *aionion kolasin*, or "age-long chastisement." The word that Jesus used for punishment is the Greek word *kolasin*, which means "remedial chastisement." The New Testament teaches that there is a remedial punishment for a limited period of time in order to bring all God's created children to repentance.

Philo, who was a Jewish philosopher contemporary with Jesus, generally used *aidion* to denote "eternal" and *aionian* to denote "temporary duration." He used the exact Greek phrase that Jesus used in Matthew 25:46 that is usually translated "eternal punishment" but should be rendered "age-long chastisement":

> It is better not to promise than not to give prompt assistance, for no blame follows in the former case, but in the latter there is dissatisfaction from the weaker class, and a deep hatred and age-long punishment [chastisement] from such as are more powerful.[21]

The translators of the Bible are sometimes strongly influenced in their work by their own personal religious beliefs, and they must keep in mind what will be accepted by the public, both of which accounts for the mistranslated phrase "eternal punishment." Not only were the books that were selected for the New Testament canon selected by imperfect men, the translation of those books is also carried out by imperfect men. As a result God's people today have a translated Bible that is profitable for training them to do good works, but it is also a Bible that can mislead them if they are not careful.

Obviously the Greek word *aion* has the same meaning in the Biblical passages that are usually translated "eternal life," and so the better translation would be "age-long life" or "life of the age to come." The *New Testament in Modern Speech* translated "eternal life" as "life of the ages." Jesus lived with and spoke to people of a different time and place who spoke in the Aramaic language. These people probably did not entertain any philosophical thoughts about "endless time," except of course for the educated Pharisees who believed in eternal punishment. To these Jews an "age-long life" in the kingdom of heaven would probably represent a long period of time that would have suited them just fine.

Although Jesus used the phrase "age-long life," which does not denote "eternity," God's people can still be assured that their spirit is eternal. Man bears the very image of God because he is spirit, as God is, and this image of God, the spiritual nature, is immortal. Also, the very notion of "limited duration" applies only to the physical universe as was discussed in Chapter One. Moreover, Paul told the Corinthians that the spirit is immortal:

> So will it be with the resurrection of the dead. The body that is sown is perishable, it is raised imperishable... For the perishable must clothe itself with the imperishable, and the mortal with immortality (1Co 15:42, 53).

The Rich Man and Lazarus

The story of the rich man and Lazarus in the book of Luke is usually portrayed as an example of how the righteous will go to heaven after death and the wicked will be sent to a hell of eternal torment. In this parable of Jesus, a rich man and a beggar both die; the rich man was buried and the beggar went to be with Abraham. The rich man looked up from hell (*Hades*) and being in torment he first asked Abraham for water to cool his tongue; he then asked to have Lazarus sent back to earth to warn the rich man's brothers of this place of torment. Abraham replied that a great gulf is fixed between Lazarus and him, preventing anyone from bringing him water, and that his brothers can read "Moses and the Prophets" if they want to avoid his fate.

On closer examination of this story it can be seen that nothing is said about the character of either the rich man or Lazarus. The rich man is not said to be wicked; he is simply described as having received good things in this life. Neither is Lazarus described as being good or righteous. Jesus simply said that he received bad things, and now the situation is reversed. The place of torment is not described as a place of punishment or a place of eternal duration, and Jesus does not say that Lazarus went to Abraham's side as a reward for righteous living. "Moses and the Prophets" say nothing about punishment after death, let alone a place of eternal torment that the rich man's brothers need to avoid, so the fate that the rich man's brothers can learn to avoid by reading the Old Testament is something other than an eternal hell. It is evident that Jesus intended this parable to teach something other than rewards and punishment after death.

What this parable does mean is not clear. One possibility is that Jesus was prophesying about the destruction of Jerusalem in AD 70, along with the end of the ruling class of Jews–the chief priests and leaders of the Sanhedrin who would be considered rich when compared to the poor, common Jews. Jesus had forewarned his followers about the coming time when there would not be left one stone upon another in Jerusalem. He also reminded them of Daniel's prophecy concerning the 490 years that would end in AD 70:

> So when you see standing in the holy place "the abomination that causes desolation," spoken of through the prophet Daniel—let the reader understand—then let those who are in Judea flee to the mountains. Let no one on the roof of his house go down to take anything out of the house. Let no one in the field go back to get his cloak. How dreadful it will be in those days for pregnant women and nursing mothers! Pray that your flight will not take place in winter or on the Sabbath. For then there will be great distress, unequaled from the beginning of the world until now—and never to be equaled again (Mt 24: 15-21).

Anyone who has read Josephus' account of the destruction of Jerusalem in AD 70 knows of the horrors that occurred there; indeed it was a "great distress" that was "never to be equaled again." The Jews who heeded Daniel's prophecy in "Moses and the Prophets" (as Abraham told the rich man) and escaped the city to flee to "Abraham's side" found safety and salvation from the Roman army. The Jewish leaders who chose to remain in Jerusalem to defend their possessions were slaughtered either by the invading Roman army or the Jewish Zealots who had taken over the city, and their corpses were probably thrown into the city's garbage heap (*Gehenna*) where they were devoured by fire and worms.

Some Christians believe that this story is actually a real event and not a parable at all which only serves to reinforce the false belief in a literal hell. If the story is real, then the "great gulf" between heaven and hell is not very wide, because the occupants on both sides can converse with each other, as the rich man did with Abraham. Moreover, the story would teach that heaven is the final abode for all poor people and hell is the ultimate destination for all rich people. The story is obviously a parable and begins as many of Jesus' parables do: there was a rich man, there was a man who had two sons, there was a landowner, etc. Here is one example:

> Then Jesus told his disciples a parable to show them that they should always pray and not give up. He said: "In a certain town there was a judge...(Lk 18:1-2).

The Old Testament says nothing about punishment after death, but there are countless warnings about the physical calamities that will befall those who live a wicked life. If God was concerned enough about the Israelites of the Old Testament to warn them of the punishments they could receive in this life, including a sudden trip to *Sheol* (an untimely death), then surely God would have included even more warnings in the Hebrew Scriptures about eternal punishment in hell if there was such a thing. The Old Testament does contain a couple references to life after death, though. The book of Genesis reports that Enoch suddenly departed this life to be with God, and in the book of Ecclesiastes we are told, "the dust returns to the ground it came from, and the spirit returns to God who gave it."

While the belief in eternal punishment was unknown among the Israelites, it was common among the ancient pagans. The Egyptians seem to be the source of most pagan religious superstitions, from whom the Greeks and Romans borrowed the basic outline for a place of eternal torment for the wicked.

The ancient Greeks believed that the universe was a sphere that was divided by a disk that was the earth. The dome above the earth was heaven, and the bottom of the great sphere was hell. Supposedly if an iron anvil was dropped from heaven it would take nine days for it to reach the flat disk of the earth, and then it would take nine more days for the anvil to fall from there to hell. Some of the terms that the pagan Greeks used for hell were *Orcus, Erebus, Tartarus,* and *Inferna,* from which we get our expression "inferno."

Greek mythology records the specific punishments of several who were condemned to Tartarus. Ixion, king of the Lapiths, for a certain monstrous sin, was bound to a wheel of fire in order to spend eternity spinning in perpetual motion. Tantalus, a mortal son of Zeus, for having attempted to deceive some of the gods who visited him by placing roasted human flesh before them, was tortured with endless hunger and thirst. He was placed in a lake up to his chin in the water, and over his head bent the branches of a tree loaded with delicious fruit. Agonizing with hunger and thirst, he stretched out his hand to seize the fruit. When it was instantly withdrawn just above his reach he stooped to drink the cool lake water, which immediately sank below his mouth, and not a drop touched his lips. When he straightened up the water rose again to his chin. From this mythological story comes our word "tantalize."

Sisyphus was condemned to roll a huge stone to the summit of a "high hill in hell," but just before he reached the top his strength would fail and the stone would roll back down to the bottom of the hill. He would be compelled to begin his labors again, always to end in the same way. Another sinner had a huge rock suspended over his head, threatening every instant to fall and crush him. Tityrus, for his crimes, was chained to a rock while a vulture fed upon his heart and entrails that reappeared as fast as they were devoured. These myths were designed to be both gruesome and everlasting.

Many of these ancient religious myths were the inventions of the rulers and priests for the purpose of governing and restraining the common people. Hence, all the early lawgivers claimed to have had communications with the gods who aided them in the preparation of their legal codes. Zoroaster, who was the founder of the Persian religion named after him, claimed to have received his laws from a divine source. Lycurgus obtained his laws from the god Apollo, Minos of Crete from Jupiter, Numa of Rome from Egeria, and Zaleucus from Minerva. The object of this fraud was to impress the minds of the multitude with religious awe in order to insure their obedience. The Christian bishop Augustine said in his book *City of God* (AD 370) that:

> This seems to have been done on no other account, but as it was the business of princes, out of their wisdom and civil prudence, to deceive the people in their religion; princes, under the name of religion, persuaded the people to believe those things true, which they themselves knew to be idle fables; by this means, for their own ease in government, tying them the more closely to civil society.[22]

Of course, in order to secure obedience, they were obliged to invent divine punishments for the disobedience of what they asserted to be divine laws. This same practice has been conducted in Christendom.

Throughout the history of Christianity the church has insisted that without the threat of eternal punishment, and without a legal code, i.e., the New Testament, people would all return to a life of sin and disobedience. What the legalists do not understand is that God does not want forced obedience from a hardened heart. He wants his created children to serve him gladly with a cheerful, circumcised heart. God's people serve under a law of faith and love, "for he who loves his fellowman has fulfilled the law" as Paul told the Roman Christians.

As already mentioned, the Hebrew Scriptures say nothing about punishment after death. Jesus and the apostles did not teach eternal punishment although a few words in the New Testament have been mistranslated to imply that. The only sources where early Christians could have learned the doctrine of eternal torment are pagan mythology, the apocryphal Book of Enoch, and the Pharisees.

Origen

Before Constantine made the church an official arm of the Roman government, Christian life was simple. Christians took care of each other and their neighbors. They avoided violence of any kind. During religious persecutions they did not revolt or fight back but went singing to the arenas where they met their deaths. It was during this time that the first great post-apostolic theologian lived. Origen published the first system of Christian theology ever framed, *De Princepiis*, in AD 230. He taught that there was no eternal punishment and that all people would eventually come to repentance. Origen had his contemporary detractors as do all religious leaders (including Mother Teresa and Billy Graham), but none of them criticized him for teaching universal salvation. Methodius, who wrote around AD 300, Pamphilus and Eusebius (AD 310), Eustathius (AD 380), Epiphanius (AD 376), Theophilus (AD 400-404), and Jerome (AD 400) all give lists of Origen's alleged errors but none mention universal salvation among them. It is in the writings of Augustine and his belief in eternal punishment for even unbaptized infants that we begin to see the influence of Roman law and mythology in mainstream Christian thinking.

Origen was born in Alexandria, Egypt about AD 185. He taught in the city for about 28 years while composing his major treatises and beginning his many critical works. While visiting in Palestine in AD 216, Origen was invited by the bishop of Jerusalem and the bishop of Caesarea to lecture in the area churches on the Bible. These same bishops ordained him a presbyter without consulting Origen's own bishop, Demetrius of Alexandria, who objected. Two synods were held at Alexandria, the first forbidding Origen to teach there and the second depriving him of his priesthood. Origen then moved to Caesarea and founded a school of literature, philosophy, and theology. During the persecutions of the Christians in AD 250 under Emperor Decius he was imprisoned and tortured. Origen was released in AD 251 but he died from his weakened condition three years later.

Origen also wrote the first major defense of Christianity, *Against Celsus*, in response to an attack on Christianity by Celsus, an Epicurean philosopher who wrote his *True Discourse* 100 years before Origen. Celsus was perhaps the first philosopher to formally criticize Christians for believing in the burning of sinners in the fires of hell. In reply to this charge, Origen wrote that such thoughts had been entertained by certain foolish Christians who were unable to see distinctly the sense of each particular passage in the Bible, or were unwilling to devote the necessary labor to the investigation of Scripture. Celsus also remarked that Christians teach that God will act the part of a cook in burning men, to which Origen replied, "not like a cook but like a God who is a benefactor of those who stand in need of discipline of fire" and "the threatened fire possesses a disciplinary, purifying quality that will consume in the sinner whatever evil material it can find to consume."[23]

An illustration of Origen's patient and intellectual manner may be seen in his reference to the attack of Celsus on the miracles of Jesus. Celsus dared not deny them since he lived only one hundred years after Jesus, and so he said, "Be it so, we accept the facts as genuine." But then he accuses Jesus of working miracles through sorcery. In reply Origen says:

> Show me the magician who calls upon the spectators of his prodigies to reform their life, or who teaches his admirers the fear of God, and seeks to persuade them to act as those who must appear before him as their judge. The magicians do nothing of the sort, either because they are incapable of it, or because they have no such desire. Themselves charged with crimes the most shameful and infamous, how should they attempt the reformation of the morals of others?

The miracles of Christ, on the contrary, all bear the impress of his own holiness, and he ever uses them as a means of winning to the cause of goodness and truth those who witness them. Thus he presented his own life as the perfect model, not only to his immediate disciples, but to all men. He taught his disciples to make known to those who heard them, the perfect will of God; and he revealed to mankind, far more by his life and works than by his miracles, the secret of that holiness by which it is possible in all things to please God. If such was the life of Jesus, how can he be compared to mere charlatans, and why may we not believe that he was indeed God manifested in the flesh for the salvation of our race?[24]

Because Origen taught that God's punishment of sinners was of a temporary nature designed to ultimately bring all of God's created children to repentance and eternal life, Christendom has for centuries declared him to be a heretic. Here is a different view presented by the historian Schaff who was once a professor at Union Theological Seminary:

> ...who, nevertheless, did more than all his enemies combined to advance the cause of sacred learning, to refute and convert heathens and heretics, and to make the church respected in the eyes of the world...Origen was the greatest scholar of his age, and the most learned and genial of all the ante-Nicene fathers. Even heathens and heretics admired or feared his brilliant talents. His knowledge embraced all departments of the philology, philosophy and theology of his day. With this he united profound and fertile thought, keen penetration, and glowing imagination. As a true divine he consecrated all his studies by prayer, and turned them, according to his best conventions, to the service of truth and piety.[25]

The Law of Love

There are several passages in the Bible that neatly summarize man's responsibility to God. Jesus summed up man's responsibility to God when he said that the commandments to love God and to love our neighbors represent the message of the entire Old Testament:

> On one occasion an expert in the law stood up to test Jesus. "Teacher," he asked, "what must I do to inherit eternal life?" "What is written in the Law?" he replied. "How do you read it?" He answered: "Love the Lord your God with all your heart and with all your soul and with all your strength and with all your mind, and Love your neighbor as yourself." "You have answered correctly," Jesus replied. "Do this and you will live" (Lk 10:25).

> So in everything, do to others what you would have them do to you, for this sums up the Law and the Prophets (Mt 7:12).

When Jesus was asked "who is my neighbor?" by the legal expert in the above passage Jesus told the parable of a Samaritan who had compassion on a man who was beaten, robbed, and left for dead. The Samaritan took care of the injured man until he recovered. Jesus gave another example of what it means to love our neighbors when he described the scene of the final judgment. The King will invite into the kingdom of heaven those who in this life gave food to those who were hungry, who gave the thirsty something to drink, who invited in the stranger, who gave clothes to the needy, who looked after the sick, and who visited those in prison. Note that Jesus *did not* say that those standing before the King will be asked if they read the Bible, belonged to a particular church, or adhered to a particular set of Bible doctrines. It is religious tradition that has imposed these constraints on Christendom.

The Jews were obligated to follow the Law of Moses in order to retain possession of the land of Israel, but God was more concerned about how the Jews treated their fellow man. The prophet Hosea said, "For I desire mercy, not sacrifice, and acknowledgment of God rather than burnt offerings (Hos 6: 6)."

Jesus quoted from this passage on two different occasions when he saw that the religious leaders were putting obedience to the law above the welfare of others. On another occasion he told the religious leaders that justice, mercy, and faithfulness were the more important matters of the law. In the grand scheme of things having compassion on those who are less fortunate completely overshadows any other commandment.

Paul agreed with Jesus that all of God's commands are summarized and fulfilled by the command to love our neighbors as ourselves:

> The commandments, "Do not commit adultery," "Do not murder," "Do not steal," "Do not covet," and whatever other commandment there may be, are summed up in this one rule: "Love your neighbor as yourself." Love does no harm to its neighbor. Therefore love is the fulfillment of the law (Ro 13:9).

The biblical writer James summarized mankind's responsibility to God by writing that pure and faultless religion is to take care of the orphans and widows in their affliction and to live morally upright lives. Paul told the Galatians to bear each other's burdens and thus fulfill the law of Christ.

God gave his commandments through Moses to a people who lived in a different world from the 21st century, a world whose societies had a natural inclination for offering animal sacrifices to deities. The majority of the commandments were designed to help the Israelites survive as a nation and retain their monotheistic beliefs. The law that governed the spiritual relationship between each Jew and God is buried among the 613 commandments of the Torah in Leviticus 19:18: "love your neighbor as yourself." When Hosea wrote, "I desire mercy, not sacrifice," he was stating that God is concerned with the showing of compassion on our neighbors rather obeying the ritualistic commandments of the old nationalistic religion of Moses.

God's last prophet, Jesus of Nazareth, taught by word of mouth and by example how this standard of love should be followed to its fullest degree. The greatest act of love, Jesus said, is to "give one's life for a friend," and this he did when he allowed himself to be crucified on the cross. That event cannot be considered a "human sacrifice," one that is offered by men to appease God; this was considered by God in the Old Testament to be abhorrent. Rather, the crucifixion was a personal sacrifice whereby Jesus voluntarily gave up his life to save the world from sin and to display the extent of God's love, thereby planting the seeds of love and repentance in the hearts of men and women. The one Jewish prophecy that best describes the life, teaching, and death of Jesus is Isaiah's description of the suffering servant. It is worth repeating here to demonstrate the minute detail of a prophecy that fits Jesus so well:

> He grew up before him like a tender shoot, and like a root out of dry ground. He had no beauty or majesty to attract us to him, nothing in his appearance that we should desire him. He was despised and rejected by men, a man of sorrows, and familiar with suffering. Like one from whom men hide their faces he was despised, and we esteemed him not.
> Surely he took up our infirmities and carried our sorrows, yet we considered him stricken by God, smitten by him, and afflicted. But he was pierced for our transgressions, he was crushed for our iniquities; the punishment that brought us peace was upon him, and by his wounds we are healed. We all, like sheep, have gone astray, each of us has turned to his own way; and the LORD has laid on him the iniquity of us all.
> He was oppressed and afflicted, yet he did not open

his mouth; he was led like a lamb to the slaughter, and as a sheep before her shearers is silent, so he did not open his mouth. By oppression and judgment he was taken away. And who can speak of his descendants? For he was cut off from the land of the living; for the transgression of my people he was stricken. He was assigned a grave with the wicked, and with the rich in his death, though he had done no violence, nor was any deceit in his mouth.

Yet it was the Lord's will to crush him and cause him to suffer, and though the LORD makes his life a guilt offering, he will see his offspring and prolong his days, and the will of the LORD will prosper in his hand. After the suffering of his soul, he will see the light of life and be satisfied; by his knowledge my righteous servant will justify many, and he will bear their iniquities. Therefore I will give him a portion among the great, and he will divide the spoils with the strong, because he poured out his life unto death, and was numbered with the transgressors. For he bore the sin of many, and made intercession for the transgressors (Isa 53:2-12).

Jesus predicted early in his ministry that he would give his life for the sins of the world. He fulfilled Isaiah's prophecy of one who would be pierced, rejected by men, and silent before his afflicters, and one who had no deceit and had done no violence. The Jewish Messiah claimants of the first century sought to overthrow the established order through violent means and all failed. In the mid 17th century a Jew by the name of Shabbetai Zevi had nearly the entire Jewish world convinced that he was their Messiah. Zevi converted to Islam, received a royal pension from the Sultan, and died ten years later, probably of natural causes. If Jesus was not the man who fulfilled this Jewish prophecy, how would it be possible for someone else to fulfill it in more detail or to a greater degree?

The apostle John believed love to be the very essence of

God and the essence of our spiritual nature. He remarked that "God is love" and he too summarized God's commandments under the command to "love one another." Paul so believed in the eternal, universal, all-encompassing nature of love that he briefly exchanged his theologian's pen for the pen of the poet when writing to the Corinthian church:

> If I speak in the tongues of men and angels, but have not love,
> I am only a resounding gong or a clanging cymbal.
> If I have the gift of prophecy
> and can fathom all mysteries and all knowledge,
> and if I have a faith that can move mountains,
> but have not love, I am nothing.
> If I give all I possess to the poor and surrender my body to the flames,
> but have not love, I gain nothing.
> Love is patient, love is kind.
> It does not envy, it does not boast, it is not proud.
> It is not rude, it is not self-seeking, it is not easily angered,
> it keeps no record of wrongs.
> Love does not delight in evil but rejoices with the truth.
> It always protects, always trusts, always hopes, always perseveres.
> Love never fails.
> But where there are prophecies, they will cease;
> where there are tongues, they will be stilled;
> where there is knowledge, it will pass away.
> For we know in part and we prophesy in part,
> but when perfection comes, the imperfect disappears.
> When I was a child, I talked like a child,
> I thought like a child, I reasoned like a child.
> When I became a man, I put childish ways behind me.

Now we see but a poor reflection as in a mirror;
then we shall see face to face.
Now I know in part; then I shall know fully, even as I
am fully known.
And now these three remain: faith, hope and love.
But the greatest of these is love.
(1Co 13).

In this moving literary masterpiece Paul explains that if we have the oratory tongue of an evangelist, or a doctorate degree in Bible Studies, or a faith in God that cannot be shaken, or a zeal for doing good works, but have not had our hearts circumcised with a compassion for others, we have wasted our time. Love seeks the welfare of others rather than being self-seeking. Love is the essence of our spiritual nature and selfishness the essence of our sinful nature. If we have compassion then we cannot fail in life. Prophecies, tongues, and knowledge are helpful but transient; when love is perfected in us then these tools become unnecessary. When we plan our lives around ourselves we are yet children. When our lives are focused on the welfare of others we have matured. Our selfishness is akin to staring at ourselves in a mirror. When our compassion for others breaks the mirror we see God facing us instead. We know so little when we ignore the plights of our neighbors; but with love we know all that is necessary, even as God knows us. We have faith in God's promises and look forward to eternal life, but compassion is the beginning and end to existence, in this world and the one to come.

The Trinity

The cornerstone teaching of the Pentateuch and the foundational belief of all Jews today is the worship of the one God, which includes the prohibition of worshiping other gods and the prohibition of making images of either God or other gods. According to the text of the Ten Commandments in both Exodus and Deuteronomy the first three commands are concerned with this fundamental principle. These three commands are preceded with the statement, "*I* am the LORD your God", and they are followed with the phrase: "*I*, the LORD your God, am a jealous God." The pronoun "I" implies one person, and this is reflected in Judaism's most important prayer which begins with "Hear, O Israel: The LORD our God, the LORD is one" which is found in Deuteronomy 6:4. The Hebrew word for "one" in this verse can in some circumstances mean one group, and some Christians point out that this "one" could refer to the Trinity. However, the entire Old Testament always portrays God with the singular "I," never with the plural "we". In Genesis 1:26 God is speaking to a subordinate, perhaps the Messiah, when he says, "Let us make man in our image."

Within the context of the Torah, then, the phrase "the LORD is one" refers to a singular deity. Jesus himself recited the "Hear, O Israel: The LORD our God, the LORD is one" just before reciting the two greatest commandments, thereby confirming his belief that God is one deity, one person, one indivisible entity. For over 3,000 years the Jews have lived by the belief taught in the Old Testament that there is only one God and that God is one. It is understandable then that Jews would find distasteful a religion that not only implicitly teaches that God is three, but that explicitly teaches that God took the form of an earthly image; images of God were strictly prohibited in the Bible.

Neither the term "Trinity," nor its concept, is explicitly found in the New Testament. One of the few times that the three persons of the Trinity are mentioned together by name is in Matthew's Gospel where Jesus told his followers to baptize disciples in the "name of the Father, and the Son, and the Holy Spirit." The term is generally believed to have been first used by Tertullian almost 200 years after the beginning of the church. Jesus never referred to himself as God. His favorite reference to himself was "the son of man." Most of the references in the four Gospels concerning the title "son of God" are instances where others called Jesus the son of God. Being the son of God does not make that person God, since the Bible calls all righteous people the "sons of God," but it would imply that Jesus is the *preeminent* son of God. When someone called Jesus "good teacher" in the gospels of Mark and Luke, Jesus replied that no one was good except God. Jesus always described himself as being subservient to God, and there was always the implication that God was a person or being apart from Jesus. According to the Gospel of John, Jesus said, "Trust in God; trust also in me."

Paul always drew a distinction between God and Jesus. On 13 occasions he used the phrase "God the Father and the Lord Jesus Christ." He told the Corinthians in this passage that while the Father is God, Jesus is the Lord:

> Yet for us there is but one God, the Father, from whom all things came and for whom we live; and there is but one Lord, Jesus Christ, through whom all things came and through whom we live (1Co 8:6).

The New Testament portrays Jesus as one who was given power and authority from God, including the power to forgive sins, and as one who was given the title "Lord." But Jesus was never said to be God.

Perhaps the strongest case for the belief that Jesus is God is found at the beginning of John's Gospel when John said that the "Word was God." Even here, the text does not explicitly say that Jesus is God. In fact, the following verse states that "he was with God in the beginning," again making a distinction between Jesus and God. The term "Word" comes from the Greek word *logos*, a very difficult if not impossible word to translate into English. John was probably explaining in a figurative and esoteric way that Jesus was with God in the beginning and that they are one in spirit and purpose.

In a wave of emotion the apostle Thomas said to Jesus, "My Lord and my God!" Considering the circumstances of finding that Jesus was resurrected from the dead, Thomas was undoubtedly forgiven of this slip. Isaiah prophesied that one would be born who would be called among other things, "mighty God" and "everlasting Father." If this passage can be used to prove that Jesus is God, then it can also be used to prove that Jesus is the Father.

The creation of the doctrine of the Trinity in the early centuries of the church was a poor attempt to reconcile the belief in monotheism with the assumed divinity of Jesus. It accomplished nothing except for pitting Christian against Christian in persecution and bloodshed. The Church also killed "heretics" over theological details such as the two natures of Jesus and whether or not the Holy Spirit proceeded from Jesus or the Father. God instilled in the Jewish people the belief that God is One, and the institutionalized Christian church has dissuaded the Jews from accepting Jesus as the son of God by implying that God is Three. Jesus himself never implied that he was God, although he believed that he and God were one in that they shared some of the same attributes. The doctrine of the Trinity should be scrapped in favor of calling Jesus by the same titles that he used for himself, Prophet, the Son of Man, the Son of God, and the Messiah, and by Paul's title of "Lord" which designates one to whom has been given power and authority.

The Church

The word "church" in the New Testament is a translation of the Greek word *ekklesia,* which means "called out." *Ekklesia* could also be translated as "assembly." The followers of Jesus are called out from the world to live morally upright lives and to help those who are in need. There was never a major distinction made in the New Testament between local churches and the "universal" church of God. All the local churches were self-governing and the only link between churches was one of mutual assistance. The universal church is described in the New Testament as a spiritual church that is nothing more than the sum total of all Jesus' followers. The purpose of the universal church of God is no different from the purpose of its individual members: to supply the spiritual and physical needs of others.

First century Christians participated in the activities of the church depending on the gifts and talents that God had given, or "appointed," to each person:

> And in the church God has appointed first of all apostles, second prophets, third teachers, then workers of miracles, also those having gifts of healing, those able to help others, those with gifts of administration, and those speaking in different kinds of tongues. Are all apostles? Are all prophets? Are all teachers? Do all work miracles? Do all have gifts of healing? Do all speak in tongues? Do all interpret? But eagerly desire the greater gifts. And now I will show you the most excellent way (1Co 12:28-31).

Some of these gifts are apparently not being "appointed" to Christians today, such as the ability to do miracles, to heal, or to speak in unfamiliar foreign languages. Many Christians however would disagree. At the end of the above passage, Paul said that he would now show the Corinthians the "most excellent way," which he does when he begins his discourse on love in chapter thirteen. Some churches believe that all Christians are to act the part of evangelists in their daily lives, citing Jesus' command to "go and make disciples of all nations." Jesus was speaking at the time, however, to his eleven disciples whom he had personally trained as evangelists over the preceding three years. Whenever Jesus spoke to crowds of ordinary people, his emphasis was always on helping people with their physical needs.

In his letters, Paul gives instructions for appointing presbyters and deacons in the Gentile churches he established. By the 4th century, when the canon of the Bible was being fixed and the term "Catholic Church" was already in use, the practice of elevating one presbyter in each church to the position of bishop had begun. Eusebius wrote in his *Ecclesiastical History* that "there should be but one bishop in a catholic church." In the church of Rome at that time Eusebius wrote that there were 47 presbyters, seven deacons, seven sub-deacons, 42 clerks, exorcists, readers, and janitors. The position of priest was later created in the church, and it was the priest who offered the perpetual sacrifice of Jesus, through the Mass, which was originally a simple memorial meal that Paul called the "Lord's Supper." The church had become a place similar to the Jewish temple where the focus was no longer on edification but on worship through sacrifices.

The function of the weekly service in each local church was originally intended to be the edification of its members. Paul makes this clear in his first letter to the Corinthians:

> On the other hand, he who prophesies speaks to men for their upbuilding and encouragement and consolation. He who speaks in a tongue edifies himself, but he who prophesies edifies the church. Now I want you all to speak in tongues, but even more to prophesy. He who prophesies is greater than he who speaks in tongues, unless some one interprets, so that the church may be edified...For you may give thanks well enough, but the other man is not edified... What then, brethren? When you come together, each one has a hymn, a lesson, a revelation, a tongue, or an interpretation. Let all things be done for edification (1Co 14:3-5, 17, 26 RSV).

Most churches today hold weekly services for the explicit purpose of offering worship to God. The edification of church members, though, was the primary reason for congregational meetings in the first century, and while worship certainly did take place during those meetings, that was not the original intent or focus.

Luke gives us a description of the activities of the first Christian church in Jerusalem:

> All the believers were together and had everything in common. Selling their possessions and goods,

they gave to anyone as he had need. Every day they
continued to meet together in the temple courts.
They broke bread in their homes and ate together
with glad and sincere hearts (Ac 2:44-46).

There is no mention made here of a weekly worship service.
The term "worship," in fact, is never used in the New Testament
in conjunction with a church service. The implication in the
New Testament is that worship is the daily performance of
good works in obedience to the command to love our neighbors
as ourselves. Paul describes Christian worship in this way:

Therefore, I urge you, brothers, in view of God's
mercy, to offer your bodies as living sacrifices, holy
and pleasing to God—this is your spiritual act of
worship (Ro 12:1).

Paul continues to the end of Romans chapter twelve
explaining that our "spiritual act of worship" is how we behave
in the world. Jesus, too, describes worship as something that
occurs outside buildings or temples:

"Our fathers worshiped on this mountain, but you
Jews claim that the place where we must worship is
in Jerusalem." Jesus declared, "Believe me, woman,
a time is coming when you will worship the Father
neither on this mountain nor in Jerusalem. You
Samaritans worship what you do not know; we
worship what we do know, for salvation is from the
Jews. Yet a time is coming and has now come when the
true worshipers will worship the Father in spirit and
truth, for they are the kind of worshipers the Father
seeks" (Jn 4: 20-23).

According to Jesus the time of worshiping in a particular
place or building had come to an end. The true worshipers
will worship in spirit and truth; they will fulfill their "spiritual

act of worship" by offering themselves as living sacrifices according to the true spiritual law, the law of love. Every time compassion is shown to one's fellow man an act of worship has been performed. Paul implied to the Colossians that everything they do is to be considered worship: "whether in word or deed, do it all in the name of the Lord Jesus, giving thanks to God the Father through him" (Col 3:17). Traditional worship is also something that is to be done continually, as in Paul's injunction to "be joyful always; pray continually; give thanks in all circumstances" (1Th 5:16-18).

The traditional forms of worship such as music, the Lord's Supper, and prayer continue to play an important part in the life of God's people. God is not in need of traditional worship and does not demand it for appeasement. What God desires is for each person to be a witness of his love by relieving some of the pain and suffering in the world.

Salvation

The spectrum of opinion on the theology of salvation is probably wider than that of any other Christian belief. At one end of the spectrum is the belief that eternal salvation comes from obedience to God's laws and commands. The Roman Catholics believe that one is saved through obedience to the Church. Some denominations believe that salvation comes from obeying the commandments in the Bible, especially the ordinance of baptism. At the other extreme is Reformed theology which teaches that no one has a free will and that God simply chooses whom he wishes to save. In-between these two extremes is the belief that salvation comes through faith apart from works of obedience. This belief has variations depending on what definition of faith is used. Some hold that simply believing that Jesus is the son of God who was resurrected from the dead is sufficient, as Paul seems to imply in Chapter Ten of his letter to the Romans. Others believe that the proper faith is acquired only when accompanied by either an emotional experience or speaking in tongues. The most important aspect of faith is unfortunately either undervalued or not mentioned at all: *repentance.*

One of the major themes of the Bible is that the Creator is a God of love, mercy, and justice. A tyrannical and despotic God should not deserve a person's allegiance or homage. It is partly for this reason that the contradictory belief in salvation apart from free will must be rejected. The arbitrary assigning of millions of souls to eternal punishment is an act that can only be ascribed to an all-powerful Hitler. Another major theme of the Bible is repentance. The Bible is one long story of God sending prophets and apostles to persuade sinners to repent of their evil ways. The idea of repentance is described in this passage from the Old Testament:

> ...and if they have a change of heart in the land where they are held captive, and repent and plead with you in the land of their conquerors and say, "We have sinned, we have done wrong, we have acted wickedly"; and if they turn back to you with all their heart and soul in the land of their enemies who took them captive...(1 Ki 8:47-48).

To repent is not just to express sorrow for having done wrong; rather it is to change one's allegiance, to change one's master, to turn from serving sin to serving God. The Greek word that we translate "repent" in the New Testament is *metanoeo*, which means to change one's mind. The gospel message of Jesus was summarized in Luke's Gospel by Jesus' pronouncement that "repentance and forgiveness of sins will be preached in his name to all nations, beginning at Jerusalem" (Lk 24:47).

To repent is to make a major spiritual decision. It is a decision born of the desire of the heart and soul to do what is right. True repentance is not a decision made simply to escape punishment. A criminal can decide to obey the civil laws and still harbor malice in his heart. This choice that each individual needs to make is illustrated by Joshua when he said to the Israelites, "choose for yourselves this day whom you will serve... as for me and my household, we will serve the Lord" (Jos 24: 15). This fundamental principle, to "serve the Lord," to declare allegiance to him and to make a commitment to obey him, is described in many different ways in the Bible. Repentance, which is one of these ways, emphasizes the beginning of one's service to God. Another word used in the Bible that describes this fundamental principle is "faith."

The new covenant is a spiritual law, the law of faith. While repentance describes the beginning of the commitment to serve God, faith describes the actual commitment itself. This commitment is a state of mind, heart, and spirit, which makes faith as different from works of obedience as night is from day. Faith will lead to obedience, but obedience will always be imperfect and off the mark since humans are imperfect. In his letter to the Romans Paul went to great lengths to explain that justification is by faith and not by obeying a written law:

> But now a righteousness from God, apart from law, has been made known, to which the Law and the Prophets testify. This righteousness from God comes through faith in Jesus Christ to all who believe (Ro 3:21-22).

This "righteousness from God," the new covenant, has been revealed to mankind "apart from law," not just the Law of Moses, but any written law. If the promise of redemption was through law, then faith would be unnecessary and the promise unattainable, or worthless, because no one can perfectly keep a written law:

> For if those who live by law are heirs, faith has no value and the promise is worthless, because law brings wrath (Ro 4:14-15).

The new covenant has always been in effect, although it was not revealed to the world until after the resurrection of Jesus. The promise of personal redemption through faith has always been extended to everyone who has ever lived. If Adam, Noah, Abraham, and Moses were not participants under the new covenant then they would not be able to partake of the promise of the new covenant, the forgiveness of sins, and eternal life. The new covenant, the law of faith, was revealed, not instituted, in Paul's day, as he tells the Ephesians:

> In reading this, then, you will be able to understand my insight into the mystery of Christ, which was not made known to men in other generations as it has now been revealed by the Spirit to God's holy apostles and prophets. This mystery is that through the gospel the Gentiles are heirs together with Israel, members together of one body, and sharers together in the promise in Christ Jesus (Eph 3:4-6).

The promise of the new covenant, which was hidden from previous generations but is now revealed to those in the post-resurrection age, is available to all of God's created children from Adam to this present time who live by faith. Paul used Abraham as an example of one who lived before the old covenant was established and before the new covenant was revealed, and Paul said that this promise of redemption, the forgiveness of sins, was fulfilled in Abraham apart from works of obedience:

> What does the Scripture say? "Abraham believed God, and it was credited to him as righteousness." Now when a man works, his wages are not credited to him as a gift, but as an obligation. However, to the man who does not work but trusts God who justifies the wicked, his faith is credited as righteousness. David says the same thing when he speaks of the blessedness of the man to whom God credits righteousness apart from works: "Blessed are they whose transgressions are forgiven, whose sins are covered" (Ro 4:3-7).

To drive home his point, Paul told the Romans that Abraham was justified at the exact moment of faith, before any obedience took place. Paul then stated that Abraham's obedience, which followed his faith, was the confirming seal of that faith:

> Is this blessedness only for the circumcised, or also for the uncircumcised? We have been saying that Abraham's faith was credited to him as righteousness. Under what circumstances was it credited? Was it after he was circumcised, or before? It was not after, but before! And he received the sign of circumcision, a seal of the righteousness that he had by faith while he was still uncircumcised. So then, he is the father of all who believe but have not been circumcised, in order that righteousness might be credited to them (Ro 4:9-11).

In the above passage Abraham is justified before he obeys God's command to be circumcised. His subsequent circumcision is evidence that he had put his faith and trust in God. If Abraham were somehow prevented from being circumcised, his failure would not nullify his faith nor his justification. His subsequent life abounded with other examples of his obedience. Moreover, Paul said that "all who believe but have not been circumcised" will be justified. Paul also told the Ephesians that salvation is through faith apart from works of obedience:

> For it is by grace you have been saved, through faith— and this not from yourselves, it is the gift of God—not by works, so that no one can boast (Eph 2:8).

Paul explained to the Galatians, too, that no one is justified by acts of obedience under a written law. Instead, redemption comes through a faith that is demonstrated by acts of love:

You who are trying to be justified by law have been alienated from Christ; you have fallen away from grace. But by faith we eagerly await through the Spirit the righteousness for which we hope. For in Christ Jesus neither circumcision nor uncircumcision has any value. The only thing that counts is faith expressing itself through love (Gal 5:4-6).

Paul's last statement in the above passage, "the only thing that counts is faith expressing itself through love," summarizes God's purpose for his people in this life. Faith in God, which begins with repentance, is expressed through showing compassion on others.

As followers of Jesus, it is his words and his teachings that are of paramount importance. In the first three Gospels Jesus spoke of salvation in terms of fulfilling God's will, with an emphasis on showing compassion on others. The Gospel of John was written in a figurative, enigmatic style, and the words of Jesus in John's Gospel are more of a paraphrase than a literal rendering. The most controversial words of Jesus come from John's gospel. Christian theology is divided over the meaning of John's enigmatic phrases such as "you must be born again" and "whoever eats my flesh and drinks my blood has eternal life." Thus, while the emphasis in the first three Gospels was on doing the will of God, John's emphasis is on believing in Jesus as the way to eternal life. The term "believe(s)" occurs over 60 times in John's Gospel. Yet, in John's Gospel, Jesus implies that to "believe in me" actually means to believe in his words and put them into practice:

If you obey my commands, you will remain in my love, just as I have obeyed my Father's commands and remain in his love. I have told you this so that my joy may be in you and that your joy may be complete. My command is this: Love each other as I have loved you. Greater love has no one than this, that he lay down his life for his friends (Jn 15:10-15).

To believe in Jesus is to obey his commands, and his command is to love each other as he loves us. This is in harmony with the emphasis of the first three Gospels, the doing of God's will, which is to love God and to love our neighbors as ourselves. Believing that Jesus died to save mankind from sin is the intended motivating factor to bring individuals to repentance, which results in putting the words of Jesus into practice:

> Therefore everyone who hears these words of mine and puts them into practice is like a wise man who built his house on the rock (Mt 7:24).

A person can hear the words of Jesus in a sermon and put them into practice without ever having read the Bible and without ever having learned who Jesus was. A God of mercy, justice, and fairness would not punish someone for not being aware of the historical details surrounding the life of Jesus. God's law for mankind is the law of faith and compassion. When we meet God face to face he can fill us in on any historical or theological details that we may have been ignorant of. In summary, the theme of spiritual salvation, throughout both the Old and New Testaments, is that of *repenting of living a selfish and sinful life, putting one's faith and trust in God, and expressing that faith through a selfless life of serving others.*

Baptism

Every church has its traditional form and theology of baptism. Some Christians believe baptism to be similar to Jewish circumcision in that infants undergo baptism as the formal entrance to the religious community. This baptism acts to remove the stain of original sin and is usually, but not always, performed by sprinkling or pouring water on the infant. Of the churches that teach adult baptism by immersion, some believe that baptism is necessary for salvation and others believe that baptism is simply a public demonstration of a newly acquired faith. Still other churches believe that Christian baptism is a baptism of the Holy Spirit that occurs without water.

As with other Bible doctrines, understanding the meaning of baptism in the New Testament is dependent on knowing the correct translation of first century Greek words, knowing when the New Testament authors were using literal or figurative speech, and knowing the historical background of the subject matter. The major themes of the Bible must always be kept in mind, so that if a literal interpretation of a passage contradicts a biblical theme it must then be assumed that a figurative meaning had been intended by the author.

The primary definition of the Greek word *baptizo*, which is translated "baptize" in our English Bibles, is "to immerse in or wash with water."[26] *Baptizo* was frequently used in antiquity to refer to dipping cloth into dye. The word *baptizo* is actually the transliterated version of the Greek word, which of course is spelled using Greek letters and so is not reproduced here. Transliteration is the process of changing the letters of a word from one language to the letters of another language.

Translators use the current dictionary definition of English words when they translate from Greek into English. The English definition of the word "baptism" is as follows:

> ...the ceremony or sacrament of admitting a person into Christianity or a specific Christian church by immersing the individual in water or by pouring or sprinkling water on the individual, as a symbol of washing away sin and of spiritual purification.[27]

It is quite obvious that the definition of the Greek word only vaguely resembles that of the English word. The question arises, "why do translators select 'baptize' as the translation of the word *baptizo* if their meanings are so different?" Indeed, the word "immerse" would be a much better translation. According to the scholar F.F. Bruce, translators continue to translate, or mistranslate, *baptizo* into English with the word "baptize" simply because this English word is entrenched in

Christian tradition. No one would buy a Bible that was bereft of "baptize." The word "baptize" is another important biblical word mistranslated in English Bibles, in addition to "hell" and "eternal."

Some churches believe that not only is water baptism necessary for salvation, but the baptism must be performed according to the meaning of the Greek word *baptizo*. In other words, the only scriptural method of baptism is that of immersion. Therefore anyone who obeys the command in an English Bible to undergo the Christian rite of church membership by pouring, sprinkling, or immersion could nevertheless be supposedly eternally lost if pouring or sprinkling was used. Apparently it would not be good enough to obey the English Bible; everyone must obey the Greek Bible with its command to be immersed. An unusual conclusion such as this is simply the result of not realizing that a major theme of the Bible is God's calling us to repentance for the forgiveness of sins. It is faith that justifies mankind, nothing more.

To understand how the first century Christians understood water baptism it is necessary to be aware of its roots in Judaism. The washing with water was used for ceremonial cleansing and purification. Jews baptized proselytes who were joining the Jewish community. All forms of washing with water were seen as being symbolic of spiritual purity. John the Baptist was a Jew and he also practiced baptism:

> And so John came, baptizing in the desert region and preaching a baptism of repentance for the forgiveness of sins. The whole Judean countryside and all the people of Jerusalem went out to him. Confessing their sins, they were baptized by him in the Jordan River (Mk 1:4-5).

John's baptism was a baptism of repentance; the repenting and baptizing were simultaneous acts. John's converts confessed their sins while being baptized, and in return they were to receive the forgiveness of sins. In accordance with the biblical theme of repentance, then, it was the act of repenting that gave John's converts the forgiveness of sins, not the baptism, which was simply one of the traditional symbolic rites of cleansing of first century Jews.

The symbolic rite of baptism, repentance, and forgiveness of sins were also linked in the minds of the first century Christians. When Peter preached his first sermon, commanding those present to repent and be baptized in order to receive the forgiveness of sins, he was obviously referring to the same "baptism of repentance for the forgiveness of sins" that was preached by John the Baptist. The repenting was traditionally done at the time of baptism, but it was the repentance and not the baptism that incurred the forgiveness of sins, as implied in these passages:

> Repent, then, and turn to God, so that your sins may be wiped out (Ac 3:19).
> God exalted him to his own right hand as Prince and Savior that he might give repentance and forgiveness of sins to Israel (Ac 5:31).
> When they heard this, they had no further objections and praised God, saying, "So then, God has granted even the Gentiles repentance unto life" (Ac 11:18).
> The Lord is not slow in keeping his promise, as some understand slowness. He is patient with you, not wanting anyone to perish, but everyone to come to repentance (2Pe 3:9).

It is this link between repentance, baptism, and forgiveness of sins that must be kept in mind when reading passages in the New Testament that refer to water baptism. Thus, when Ananias told Paul to "Get up, be baptized and wash your sins away," it would have been understood in the minds of first century Christians that the forgiveness of Paul's sins was due to his repenting during the act of baptism, and not due to his getting wet. The only difference that can be ascertained between John's baptism and that of the apostles' in the New

Testament is that the apostles "baptized into the name of the Lord Jesus" (Ac 19:5).

There is a tendency among some churches to automatically associate every occurrence of the word "baptism" in the New Testament with water baptism unless the immediate text obviously refers otherwise. Paul frequently uses "baptize" as a metaphor, such as when he tells the Corinthians that the Israelites "were all baptized into Moses in the cloud and in the sea." What is interesting about this passage is that those who were baptized had passed through the sea without getting wet. The ones who were not baptized, the Egyptians, were fatally immersed in the sea.

Paul also uses the expressions "baptized into Christ" and "baptized into one body." There is no question that Paul is at least alluding to water baptism in these expressions, but his point is that the Christian has "joined" with the body of Christ, with "baptized" being a metaphor for the act of being joined. In Romans Chapter Six Paul uses another metaphor in the same immediate context as that of "baptized" when he explains how the Christian's sinful nature has been "crucified." On three other occasions Paul uses "crucified" as a metaphor in the same way. Paul's point is that the Christian who is spiritually joined (baptized) with Christ has spiritually killed (crucified) the sinful nature. There is no physical baptizing or crucifying occurring here. And, in keeping with Paul's theme of justification by faith in his letter to the Romans, the Christian is "baptized into Christ" at the moment of faith (repentance).

A favorite passage used to support the doctrine of salvation by water baptism is found in John's Gospel:

> In reply Jesus declared, "I tell you the truth, no one can see the kingdom of God unless he is born again." "How can a man be born when he is old?" Nicodemus asked. "Surely he cannot enter a second time into his mother's womb to be born!" Jesus answered, "I tell you the truth, no one can enter the kingdom of God unless he is born of water and the Spirit. Flesh

gives birth to flesh, but the Spirit gives birth to spirit.
You should not be surprised at my saying, 'You must
be born again.' The wind blows wherever it pleases.
You hear its sound, but you cannot tell where it comes
from or where it is going. So it is with everyone born
of the Spirit" (Jn 3:3-8).

It is a stretch to say that this passage supports the necessity
of water baptism since the word "baptism" does not even appear
in this text. However, the word "water" does appear here, which
supposedly refers to baptism. But this is highly unlikely. The
primary point of this text is that a person must be born again
which means being born of the Spirit. Jesus said that the Spirit
gives birth to spirit, and then says, "So it is with everyone born
of the Spirit." It would be contradictory and confusing for Jesus
to say that being born again includes both the water and the
Spirit, then afterwards say that being born again includes only
the Spirit.

When Jesus said that a person must be born of water
and the Spirit, he was answering Nicodemus' question about
how someone could be born twice. In effect, Jesus was telling
Nicodemus that, no, a person is not born twice physically, but
once physically and once spiritually. Jesus even elaborates on this
fact in his following statement when he says, "flesh gives birth
to flesh, but the Spirit gives birth to spirit." In summary, Jesus
began by telling Nicodemus that a person must be born again
(by the Spirit), Nicodemus then gets the discussion sidetracked
by asking if a man can be physically born twice, Jesus explains
that, yes, we are born twice, once by flesh (water), and once
by the Spirit, and finally Jesus gets back to his original point
of the necessity of being born again, by the Spirit. As to why
Jesus would use the term "water" to refer to the physical birth,
it must simply be recalled that all infants are born from a sac of
embryonic fluid, which is essentially water. To be born again,
by the Spirit, simply means that a person receives a spiritual
awakening when the law of the Spirit, the law of faith and love,
is allowed to work in that person. In other words, repentance
gives birth to works of love.

New Testament baptism can only be properly understood when placed in context with the biblical themes of justification by faith, repentance for the forgiveness of sins, and the justice and mercy of God. Concerning this last theme, a loving God would not eternally punish anyone for failing to get wet. Repentance always leads to an imperfect obedience, since all men are imperfect, and not all repentant people will be aware of the command to be baptized, let alone be aware of the meaning of the Greek words.

The End Times

The study of last things, eschatology (Greek-*eschatos*) has produced a myriad of theories about biblical prophecies concerning future events. The prophets of the Old Testament spoke of "the day of Yahweh" when God would overthrow the Jews' enemies and begin a messianic age. Christian theories differ according to whether prophecies are to be taken literally or symbolically (especially in John's Book of Revelation) and whether or not biblical prophecies have already been fulfilled. Most Christians are looking forward to the second coming (the Parousia) of Jesus Christ.

Those who interpret the prophecies in Revelation as mostly symbolic believe that those prophecies apply to all of the trials and tribulations of the last two thousand years. Others interpret John's vision for the most part literally, believing that we are approaching a seven-year tribulation period during which the "antichrist" will appear. Sometime during this period (beginning, middle, or end) all the Christians will disappear from the face of the earth and meet Jesus in the air as he comes to receive them (his second coming). This is popularly known as the "rapture," a Latin term which means "caught up" and which is a translation from the Greek in 1 Thessalonians 4:17. This sudden disappearance will supposedly result in catastrophes caused by drivers disappearing from their vehicles and pilots disappearing from their planes, etc. After the tribulation period

Jesus is supposed to come back to Earth a third time and reign for a thousand years. Then the Battle of Armageddon takes place after which there will be a new heavens and a new earth. Those who believe that the New Testament prophecies have not yet been fulfilled hold a "Futurist" viewpoint.

There is a biblical eschatological theme that runs through all New Testament prophecies and which is completely ignored by most Christians; the 1st century imminency of the fulfillment of all remaining prophecy. Many of the Christians' critics are aware of this theme and use it to show that the New Testament is in error because the prophecies were apparently not fulfilled in the 1st century as the first Christians said and believed they would be. Not only do Christians ignore the emphatic statements made by Jesus and his followers concerning the fact that the fulfillment of the prophecies was "at hand," they also ignore the historical events surrounding the destruction of Jerusalem in AD 70 that fulfill many of these prophecies. The belief that the New Testament prophecies were fulfilled in the 1st century is referred to as the "Preterist" viewpoint. A partial Preterist believes that all prophecy except for the return of Jesus has been fulfilled, while the full Preterist believes that Jesus returned in the 1st century. Jesus spoke of the tribulation that was about to come, and his second coming, both of which would happen in the lifetime of his listeners:

> When you are persecuted in one place, flee to another. I tell you the truth, you will not finish going through the cities of Israel before the Son of Man comes (Mt 10:23).
> I tell you the truth, some who are standing here will not taste death before they see the Son of Man coming in his kingdom" (Mt 16:28).
> I tell you the truth, this generation will certainly not pass away until all these things have happened (Mt 24: 34).
> "Yes, it is as you say," Jesus replied. "But I say to all of you: In the future you will see the Son of Man sitting

at the right hand of the Mighty One and coming on the clouds of heaven" (Mt 26:64).

For this is the time of punishment in fulfillment of all that has been written (Lk 21:22).

Jesus turned and said to them, "Daughters of Jerusalem, do not weep for me; weep for yourselves and for your children. For the time will come when you will say, 'Blessed are the barren women, the wombs that never bore and the breasts that never nursed!' Then they will say to the mountains, 'Fall on us!' and to the hills, 'Cover us!' (Lk 23:30).

Jesus answered, "If I want him to remain alive until I return, what is that to you? You must follow me" (Jn 21:22).

In the above passages Jesus told his listeners that they would not be done evangelizing when he returned, that all prophecies would be fulfilled in their generation, that they (his listeners) would see him returning on the clouds of heaven, that in their lifetime all that was written would be fulfilled, that they (his listeners) would experience a time of tribulation, and that John would remain alive until he returned.

Paul spoke with the expectancy of Jesus coming in his lifetime:

And do this, understanding the present time. The hour has come for you to wake up from your slumber, because our salvation is nearer now than when we first believed. The night is nearly over; the day is almost here. So let us put aside the deeds of darkness and put on the armor of light (Ro 13:11-12).

The God of peace will soon crush Satan under your feet. The grace of our Lord Jesus be with you (Ro 16:20).

What I mean, brothers, is that the time is short. From now on those who have wives should live as if they had none; those who mourn, as if they did not;

those who are happy, as if they were not; those who buy something, as if it were not theirs to keep; those who use the things of the world, as if not engrossed in them. For this world in its present form is passing away (1Co 7:29-31).

These things happened to them as examples and were written down as warnings for us, on whom the fulfillment of the ages has come (1Co 10:11).

Listen, I tell you a mystery: We will not all sleep, but we will all be changed—in a flash, in the twinkling of an eye, at the last trumpet. For the trumpet will sound, the dead will be raised imperishable, and we will be changed (1Co 15:51-52).

In the sight of God, who gives life to everything, and of Christ Jesus, who while testifying before Pontius Pilate made the good confession, I charge you to keep this command without spot or blame until the appearing of our Lord Jesus Christ (1Ti 6:13-14).

According to the Lord's own word, we tell you that we who are still alive, who are left till the coming of the Lord, will certainly not precede those who have fallen asleep. For the Lord himself will come down from heaven, with a loud command, with the voice of the archangel and with the trumpet call of God, and the dead in Christ will rise first. After that, we who are still alive and are left will be caught up together with them in the clouds to meet the Lord in the air. And so we will be with the Lord forever (1Th 4:15-17).

May God himself, the God of peace, sanctify you through and through. May your whole spirit, soul and body be kept blameless at the coming of our Lord Jesus Christ (1Th 5:23).

Other New Testament writers fully believed that they were living in the "last days" and that the "end of all things" was at hand:

No, this is what was spoken by the prophet Joel: "In the last days, God says, I will pour out my Spirit on all people" (Ac 2:16-17).

In the past God spoke to our forefathers through the prophets at many times and in various ways, but in these last days he has spoken to us by his Son...(Heb 1:1-2).

For in just a very little while, "He who is coming will come and will not delay (Heb 10:37).

Be patient, then, brothers, until the Lord's coming. See how the farmer waits for the land to yield its valuable crop and how patient he is for the autumn and spring rains. You too, be patient and stand firm, because the Lord's coming is near (Jas 5:7-8).

The end of all things is near. Therefore be clear minded and self-controlled so that you can pray (1Pe 4:7).

He was chosen before the creation of the world, but was revealed in these last times for your sake (1Pe 1:20).

Dear children, this is the last hour; and as you have heard that the antichrist is coming, even now many antichrists have come. This is how we know it is the last hour (1Jn 2:18).

According to John, all the events in the Book of Revelation were to happen soon:

The revelation of Jesus Christ, which God gave him to show his servants what must soon take place...Blessed is the one who reads the words of this prophecy, and blessed are those who hear it and take to heart what is written in it, because the time is near (Rev 1:1,3).

I am coming soon. Hold on to what you have, so that no one will take your crown (Rev 3:11).

"Behold, I am coming soon! Blessed is he who keeps the words of the prophecy in this book" (Rev 22:7).

"Behold, I am coming soon! My reward is with me,

and I will give to everyone according to what he has done (Rev 22:12).

He who testifies to these things says, "Yes, I am coming soon." Amen. Come, Lord Jesus (Rev 22:20).

The Futurists' explanation for these many references to the immediate fulfillment of prophetic events is that these references are referring to God's time. To God a thousand years is as a day according to Peter, and so a thousand years would be "soon" for God. Of course, to God, for whom time does not exist, a billion years would also be "soon," so there would be no purpose to or meaning in relating prophetic events to God's time. The very fact that there are so many instances of different biblical writers stating that the New Testament prophetic events were imminent indicates that this imminency is a major eschatological theme in the Bible. In view of the fact that there is no mention in the Bible about Jesus returning to earth *thousands of years* in the future, there is simply no reason for not accepting at face value the dozens of references to the immediate fulfillment in the 1st century of the tribulation events and the return of Jesus. Moreover, the Bible distinguishes between the distant future and imminency:

"The vision of the evenings and mornings that has been given you is true, but seal up the vision, for it concerns the distant future" (Da 8:26).

Then he told me, "Do not seal up the words of the prophecy of this book, because the time is near (Rev 22:10).

Daniel was told to seal up his vision because it concerned the "distant future" (490 years) whereas John was told not to seal up his vision because the time was "near." In biblical language, then, "near" must be substantially less than 490 years.

The most complete description of the "end times" in plain language is found in Matthew Chapter 24. Jesus began by telling his disciples that the buildings in Jerusalem would be completely torn down. This, of course, occurred in AD 70 at the end of the Jewish war with the Romans. When his disciples asked when these events, including his second coming, would occur, Jesus gave them a long list of signs, all of which happened in the 1st century:

- False Christs and false prophets will appear – In his first epistle John wrote that false prophets and antichrists were already in the world.
- There will be wars and nation will rise against nation – The Jewish war with the Romans involved the entire Middle East.
- There will be famines and earthquakes – Luke reported that there was a severe famine throughout the Roman world during the reign of Claudius (Acts 11:28). The Jewish war itself created famines in many cities according to Josephus. In his history *The Twelve Caesars,* Suetonius (AD 69-AD 140) reported that earthquakes were a common occurrence in the 1st century.
- The gospel will be preached in the whole world – In the 1st century, historians referred to the Roman Empire as the "whole world." Paul told the Romans that their faith was being reported "all over the world" (Rom 1:8). Jesus told his apostles that *they* would be his witnesses "to the ends of the earth" (Acts 1:8). Paul told the Colossians that "this is the gospel that you heard and that has been proclaimed to every creature under heaven" (Col 1:23).
- The "abomination that causes desolation" will be standing in the holy place – As mentioned in Chapter Two, Jesus is referring to Daniel's prophecy which was fulfilled in AD 70 when the Romans brought their pagan standards into the Jewish temple.
- There will be great distress – Over one million Jews, men, women and children, lost their lives in the Jewish war.

John wrote in Revelation that the "beast," which Christians frequently associate with the antichrist that John wrote about in his epistles, was identified by the number "666" which was the number of his name (Rev 13:17-18). It was a common practice in the 1st century to calculate the numbers of people's names, this being possible because the alphabet letters of Hebrew, Greek, and Latin also served for numbers. The letters of a name that also served as numbers could be added up to arrive at the "number" for that name. The Roman Emperor who ruled during most of the Jewish war, who pushed for recognition as God more than any other Emperor, and who was the cruelest and most degenerate of the Roman Emperors was Nero. The numbers in his Latin name add up to "666." Nero blamed the AD 64 fire in Rome on the Christians and subjected many of them to cruel deaths. Some were crucified, some were covered with the skins of animals and left to be devoured by dogs, and some were used as human torches at night.

When the signs listed above had been fulfilled, Jesus told his disciples not to believe reports of his second coming yet. There were still a few signs that were to appear. He obviously implied that some of the disciples would still be alive at the time the signs occurred in order for them to be able to ignore false reports of his second coming. Jesus then told them that when they see these latter signs they will know that the end is near, "right at the door." To make it perfectly clear that the "end times" would occur in their lifetime, Jesus finished his prophecy by saying "this generation will certainly not pass away until all these things have happened."

Most of the "end times" signs were fulfilled by AD 70, but it was not yet time for Jesus' second coming. His disciples were not to believe false reports of his appearance. Jesus told them that immediately after the distress, or tribulation (the Jewish war), the sun and moon would be darkened, the stars would fall from the sky and the heavenly bodies would be shaken. These were the final signs. It is at this time that the Son of Man would "appear in the sky" and return "coming on the clouds of the sky" (Mt 24:30). Jesus said that these signs would occur during the disciples' generation. In her remarkable book, *Prophecy Paradox: The Case for a First Century End Time*, Lynn Louise Schuldt documents in minute detail how the eruption of Mount Vesuvius in AD 79 fulfilled the final signs of Jesus' prophecy. The historical records that survive from the 1st century describe how the ash from the volcano blotted out the sun and moon across the Roman Empire. The drifting clouds of ash would have made the stars at night appear to be moving, or "falling." Showers of flaming rock spewed from the volcano would also give the appearance of falling stars and shaking heavenly bodies. Jesus said his appearance would be "as lightening." Volcanic eruptions are frequently accompanied by lightening, including the Mount St. Helen's eruption in 1980. When the remaining disciples were "caught up" in the air to meet Jesus, they would have left their dead bodies behind since "the dust returns to the ground it came from, and the spirit returns to God who gave it" (Ecc 12:7). This would explain Jesus' remark that "wherever there is a carcass, there the vultures will gather" (Mt 24:28). Those who remained on earth would undoubtedly have attributed the sudden deaths of Jesus' disciples to the strange events caused by the volcano, which included the burying of Pompeii, a town that had been seriously damaged by an earthquake in AD 63. John wrote that "every eye will see him" when Jesus returns, but only his disciples would have recognized him for who he was.

The Book of Revelation has frequently been dated to the reign of Domitian (AD 81-96) which would place its writing after the events of AD 70 and AD 79, thereby eliminating those events as the fulfillment of John's prophecies. This dating, however, is based almost solely on a statement from the writings of Irenaeus that date to the late 2nd century. The preponderance of evidence, as already seen, is in favor of John having written his Apocalypse during the reign of Nero (AD 54-68) when all of Jesus' "end times" signs were about to be fulfilled. Moreover, Nero was the sixth of the Roman Emperors, and at the time of the writing of Revelation John said that there were "also seven kings. Five have fallen, one is, the other has not yet come; but when he does come, he must remain for a little while"

(Rev 17:10). Therefore Nero was the reigning Emperor (king) when John wrote Revelation. Julius Caesar was a dictator who had never been crowned Emperor. Even if he is counted as one of the five fallen kings, that would put the writing of Revelation in the time frame of AD 41-54 during the reign of Claudius.

Many Futurists argue that to claim that Jesus has already returned to Earth is to take away the hope of the Christian. In other words, the Christian no longer has anything to look forward to. However, the hope of the redeemed is eternal life with the Lord, and this hope is fulfilled when we leave this earthly existence, whether it be by a natural death or by Jesus returning in a visible form. A drawback to believing that Jesus will return again in our near future is the tendency to sit on one's hands waiting for his return and thereby neglect one's God-given responsibilities in this world, which is the subject of the next chapter.

Chapter Six

Applying the Bible

The average person's worldview is never large enough to allow this life to be put in the proper perspective and to properly prioritize the details of life. Eternity is usually comprehended as nothing more than an intellectual fact that is kept filed away in one's memory. The problems of the world absorb the average person's attention and prevent him or her from understanding the real purpose that God has given to each person. Everyone has been placed into this physical world for, relatively speaking, a few moments–with the mission of relieving some of the suffering being experienced by others. When those few moments have passed, the body "returns to the ground it came from, and the spirit returns to God who gave it." The correct perspective of reality is that of a spiritual eternity with this physical life being nothing more than the first day of eternity.

God's purpose for mankind was introduced to the world in two stages. God began by using the Jewish people to inform the world that he is a loving God and that all other so-called gods are non-existent. This task has been for the most part accomplished and so the need for a theocracy and a written religious law has disappeared. The fact that the Book of the Covenant has been lost for thousands of years is indicative that God is no longer concerned with anyone's adherence to it.

The second stage began when the seed that was planted in the Mosaic Law, the command to "love your neighbor as yourself," began to bloom in the first century when God's last and greatest prophet, the suffering servant Jesus, proclaimed that this command is the summation of religious law. In the following century Jews began to implement this principle of love when after the war of AD 135 they renounced violence completely as a means of settling their differences with the Gentiles. It was at this time that Judaism ceased to be a national religion, with the emphasis shifting to the study and observance of the Torah. Slavery disappeared among the Jews with the realization that all men are equally made in God's image. Not until the 20th century do they again take up arms as a nation.

Just as the Jews put down the sword, Christians took up the sword when the church became a political/religious institution. Violence was made a tool of the church under Augustine's "total Christian society" theology, in which the church was to use force to convert the heathen and to reform the Christian heretics. This barbaric policy was carried out on a grand scale with the Crusades of the 11th, 12th and 13th centuries. The Popes encouraged the organizing of huge armies of poor peasants (mobs would be more accurate) to be sent to rescue Jerusalem from the Moslems. These frenzied mobs killed everyone and destroyed everything in their path, regardless of religious beliefs. The persecution of Jews by Christians began around the middle of the first millennium and continued into the 20th century.

The Protestant Reformation continued the Christian use of violence as a means of attaining spiritual ends. Both Martin Luther and John Calvin approved of the killing of their religious enemies. The Jews were persecuted and killed by all the major Christian parties. The only reforming done was to exchange a Catholic dogma for a Protestant one. The only voice of reason and compassion during this time was that of Erasmus and the religious humanists. He pleaded for all religious parties to put down the sword and to proclaim freedom of religion and freedom of thought for every individual. Both Catholics and Protestants hated him for his pacifism.

The lack of compassion breeds hate, which always seems

to be directed towards anyone who is different, whether the difference be in culture, religion, or race. The United States persecuted American Indians and enslaved Africans. During World War II there were few Christians worldwide who were genuinely concerned with the mass killing of Jews, the Final Solution of Hitler. Strict immigration regulations in the United States and British-controlled Palestine prevented thousands of Jews from fleeing certain death in Europe. In spite of this, it was with a major contribution from two Jews, Albert Einstein and Robert Oppenheimer, on the atomic bomb project, that World War II in the Pacific was brought to an abrupt end, saving perhaps 100,000 lives of both Americans and Japanese by canceling the plans to invade the island of Japan. No country is immune from the hate of others, as seen in the terrorist attacks on New York City and Washington DC on September 11, 2001, which may have been, in part, revenge for the Persian Gulf War. The bombing of the Federal Building in Oklahoma City was revenge for the violence and deaths that occurred in Waco, Texas. It is a fact of history and a fact of human nature that violence breeds more violence.

Selfishness breeds materialism, unbridled ambition, and infidelity, the moral flaws which when allowed to flourish in families result in the abandonment of the training and development of children. This results in generations of young adults with no sense of right and wrong who turn to crime to solve their problems. Yet, civilization has made progress. Personal freedom and human rights are more widespread now than ever before. The totalitarian regime of the Soviet Union has fallen.

The worldview of many people is molded by the spirit of selfishness. Their thoughts and energies revolve around getting a better job, a bigger house, and a newer car. Many people attend church a couple times a week thinking that this will ensure their eternal future. This is an upside-down worldview that completely ignores the teachings of Jesus, especially in his Sermon on the Mount. Jesus taught that an individual's focus is to be on people, not things, and on the present day, not on next week or next year. Mankind has been put on earth for a brief time to fulfill a mission: lending a helping hand on a daily basis to those who are in need.

In his Sermon on the Mount Jesus described a sacrificial love for others that prohibits retaliation against one's enemies. Moreover, God's people are to love their enemies and use compassion to lead them to repentance. The process begins with God's love transforming the heart and kindling the passion for love therein. Love is infectious. John said, "we love, because he first loved us." He also implied that if we hate others, God will not accept our love for him:

> If anyone says, "I love God," yet hates his brother, he is a liar. For anyone who does not love his brother, whom he has seen, cannot love God, whom he has not seen. And he has given us this command: Whoever loves God must also love his brother (1Jn 4:20-21).

The law of Christ is a state of heart and mind that determines how others are to be treated, regardless of the social or civil implications. There is no law or principle that overrides this spiritual law:

> But the fruit of the Spirit is love, joy, peace, patience, kindness, goodness, faithfulness, gentleness and self-control. Against such things there is no law (Gal 5: 22-23).

The teachings of Jesus are frequently made to apply as an ideal only for one-on-one confrontations with others and not when acting as members of society in which support may be required for capital punishment and "just wars." Christians who support capital punishment and war appeal to the examples of the Israelites in the Old Testament. Capital punishment was part of the Law of Moses, and God supposedly led the Israelites into battle against their enemies. As mentioned earlier, the Law of Moses was for a theocracy and for a people who lived in an age when violence was an accepted, integral part of society. No one wishes to re-institute a body of laws that stipulates the death sentence for children who curse their parents and for anyone who works on the Sabbath.

The Israelites were a chosen people for whom God had formulated civil laws, making their government a theocracy. God's people, whether Jew or Gentile, no longer live in a theocracy and are not called upon to police the world. Moreover, Jesus distinctly contrasted his teachings with the Law of Moses. Jesus summarized Moses' civil laws with the phrase "eye for eye and tooth for tooth" and then said, "But I tell you, do not resist an evil person. If someone strikes you on the left cheek, turn to him the other also." Likewise, Jesus described the Israelites' "just war" practices with the phrase "love your neighbor and hate your enemies" and then proceeded to explain that now God's people are to "love your enemies and pray for those who persecute you."

The objections to accepting the law of Christ as the norm in every situation are many. Are we not abrogating our civic responsibilities by not supporting the capital punishment laws of our country? Are we not encouraging the disintegration of society by not helping to keep the criminals at bay? The Bible answers these questions by describing the Christian's relationship to the government and to the world in general. Paul implies in his letter to the Romans that the governing authorities and the church are distinctly separate spheres of influence in this world because rulers live by the sword:

> Everyone must submit himself to the governing authorities, for there is no authority except that which God has established. The authorities that exist have been established by God. Consequently, he who rebels against the authority is rebelling against what God has instituted, and those who do so will bring judgment on themselves. For rulers hold no terror for those who do right, but for those who do wrong. Do you want to be free from fear of the one in authority?

Then do what is right and he will commend you. For he is God's servant to do you good. But if you do wrong, be afraid, for he does not bear the sword for nothing. He is God's servant, an agent of wrath to bring punishment on the wrongdoer. Therefore, it is necessary to submit to the authorities, not only because of possible punishment but also because of conscience. This is also why you pay taxes, for the authorities are God's servants, who give their full time to governing (Ro 13:1-6).

Paul depicts the authorities as being special servants of God who operate outside the spiritual law of Christ. The ruler is supposedly God's "agent of wrath" who bears a sword. It would be contrary to God's merciful nature for him to specifically appoint tyrannical rulers such as Hitler to leadership positions, so Paul must be interpreted as saying that God allows the governing authorities to exist and that God's people are to submit to these authorities except when asked to do something that is contrary to the teachings of Jesus. Christians are not forbidden to participate in government, but at the same time they are to abide by the law of Christ in all situations, which would forbid them from holding many governmental positions. Jesus did not tell the tax collectors and soldiers to leave their positions in government, but rather he told them to "collect no more than what is appointed for you" and "do not intimidate anyone or accuse falsely, and be content with your wages" (Lk 3:13-14).

Yet law enforcement and the military are certainly forms of public service. Public protection sometimes results in officers paying the ultimate sacrifice. Many believe that they are called to participate in law enforcement, which from a moral standpoint is perhaps the most difficult of occupations. The detaining and removing of criminals from society by a Christian must be balanced with showing compassion to those same criminals. Good law enforcement officers are extremely reluctant to use deadly force. Many believe that criminals do not deserve sympathy, but few criminals simply choose one day to live a life of crime. The vast majority of them were bred to be criminals by growing up in neglect and abuse where the only role model was the local gang. It is easier to have compassion on criminals when they are viewed as victims of their environment. Many criminals have repented and become model citizens. In the final analysis, though, the duties and responsibilities of law enforcement and the military are not compatible with the principles of the law of Christ.

As spiritual beings who are temporarily confined to this physical existence, God's people are "aliens and strangers in the world," as Peter puts it. Paul says that our "citizenship is in heaven," and though we live in this world, we are "not of the world." The Christian's purpose in this world is to fulfill the physical and spiritual needs of others, either on a one-to-one basis or by pooling resources with others. During the first three centuries Christians did not resist their persecutors or actively demonstrate against the government. After Constantine became the ruler of the Roman Empire the purpose of the church began to change as the church entered into a partnership with the Roman government. No longer was the church in the world but not of the world; the church became an institution and merged with the world as the religious arm of the Roman Empire.

Paul told the Corinthians, "If anyone destroys God's temple, God will destroy him; for God's temple is sacred, and you are that temple" (1Co 3:17). Some might argue that "God's temple" refers only to the Christian, but who knows whether or not the person who is killed in a "just war" or the electric chair is a Christian. Moreover, anytime a human life is taken, all future opportunity in this life for that person to come to repentance is taken as well. Since the body is God's temple each person has an obligation to take proper care of it both physically and emotionally through proper nutrition, rest, and relaxation. This is not an end in itself; a person is more capable of helping others if he or she is healthy.

Considering the short time spent on earth and the mission

of helping those in need, God's people should not be overly concerned with the acquiring and retaining of so-called "God-given" rights such as life, liberty, and the pursuit of happiness. Each person is to be focused on the God-given mission of helping others by using the time, talents, abilities, and resources that are supplied by God. Jesus taught that no one should worry about the physical necessities of life; instead, his followers are to "seek first his kingdom and his righteousness, and all these things will be added to you" (Mt 6:33). Persecution and death are not to be considered calamities. As Paul said, "To live is Christ and to die is gain." Death itself is nothing more than the separation of the body from the mind or spirit: "To be absent from the body is to be present with the Lord." Regarding one's station in life Paul said,

> Were you a slave when you were called? Don't let it trouble you-although if you can gain your freedom, do so...each man, as responsible to God, should remain in the situation God called him to (1Co 7:21).

If a person can improve his or her position in life without contradicting Jesus' teachings, then that is permissible. God's people are not told in the Bible to defend their civil rights; rather they are warned that, "everyone who wants to live a godly life in Christ Jesus will be persecuted." When Paul became a believer he gave up his personal rights:

> But whatever was to my profit I now consider loss for the sake of Christ. What is more, I consider everything a loss compared to the surpassing greatness of knowing Christ Jesus my Lord, for whose sake I have lost all things (Php 3:8).

Not even our bodies belong to us, for Paul asks, "Do you not know that your body is a temple of the Holy Spirit, who is in you, whom you have received from God? You are not your own; you were bought at a price" (1Co 6:19-20). It would seem that we have no personal rights in regard to our bodies since they belong to God; this would imply that we do not have the right to take either our own life or the life of unborn children by abortion.

It is normal human behavior to want to rationalize the Sermon on the Mount by claiming it is contrary to good reason and common sense to apply the teachings of Jesus to all situations. Pacifism is generally regarded as a weakness. It is part of human nature to seek an "eye for eye," to punish wrongdoers, and to defend one's community and country; it is easy to give in to this impulse. On the other hand, to exercise restraint and return evil with good requires patience, self-control, spiritual maturity, and faith in the fact that God has taken responsibility for governing the nations. The word "meek" is not a popular word, yet Jesus said, "blessed are the meek." The law of Christ that tells Christians to love their enemies in all situations is a theme found throughout the New Testament. There are no commands or examples in the New Testament that indicate otherwise. The incident of Jesus driving the moneychangers from the temple is more accurately depicted as Jesus driving out their animals with the moneychangers in quick pursuit: "he made a whip out of cords, and drove all from the temple area, both sheep and cattle" (Jn 2:15). There is no question that loving an enemy is difficult, hence the expression "the hard sayings of Jesus." The law of Christ is an ideal, a goal that everyone should work towards with the understanding that no one will ever be able to fulfill this law to the degree that Jesus did. His compassion was great enough to enable him to ask God to forgive those who had crucified him.

It is sometimes difficult to understand how the first Christians were able to live according to the teachings of Jesus without exceptions and without any apparent concern for their own welfare. Most of the apostles were persecuted and killed for preaching the Gospel. Perhaps they understood the extremely short duration of this life when compared to eternity. James put it well when he said, "What is your life? You are a mist that appears for a little while and then vanishes" (Jas 4:14). One's physical life is but a second on eternity's clock. As this becomes more apparent, each person's problems and discomforts become more trivial. The more the mind is focused on spiritual things the easier it becomes to live according to the law of Christ. Of the enemies of the cross of Christ Paul said that, "Their mind is on earthly things. But our citizenship is in heaven" (Php 3:20). God's people have been sent to earth on a weekend business trip with a temporary visa to fulfill a mission. There are hundreds of ways for a person to help those in the community who are in need, depending on the talents and interests of that person. Some examples of public and private service would include teaching, the medical profession, foster care, volunteer organizations, firefighting, visiting those in prison and nursing homes, and donating blood, food, and clothing.

For those who strive to be holy, life is a battle between the spiritual nature and the human/sinful nature, between compassion and hate, and between selflessness and selfishness. The more God's people practice compassion, the more natural it becomes and the more zealous they become to relieve the sufferings of others. We were made in the image of God and it is the desire of our spiritual nature to conform to that image, to allow the love of God in us to subdue our selfish nature so that we can pass that love on to others. God first calls us to repent and to change the direction of our life from sin to service. Thereafter we are to treat each day as a day of repentance whereby we strive moment by moment to turn from selfishness to selflessness. This can only be accomplished by focusing on one day at a time while walking hand-in-hand with God.

Epilogue

It is a reasonable assumption that God wants mankind to know the difference between truth and religious traditions—hence the necessity of exploring the origins of the Bible. Human history is riddled with false religious beliefs, the geocentric theory of the universe being one prime example of a tradition that has been discovered to be incorrect. Even in this modern era it is still necessary to apply historical facts and sound reasoning to all remaining religious traditions in order to prove their veracity. It is also necessary to have a trust in God that allows the Bible student to be content with the truth that remains after such an investigation is complete.

It has been the habit of every great religion to collect and preserve the writings of its spiritual leaders. This is necessary for a religion's survival. God's message for mankind has been transmitted over the centuries buried in the books of the Judeo-Christian tradition. That message leaps out from the pages when the Bible is read as God intended, as a history of God's prophets and apostles rather than as a legal code of commandments and dogma. The Bible should be used, according to Paul, as a guide that is *useful* for preparing the people of God to do *every good work*. If each individual realigns his or her priorities in life with the law of faith and love, the 21st century may see significant progress towards a more compassionate world.

Endnotes

1. Will Durant, *The Reformation* (Simon and Schuster, 1957), p. 858.
2. Ibid., p. 858.
3. Will and Ariel Durant, *The Age of Reason Begins* (Simon and Schuster, 1961), p. 609.
4. Ibid., p. 608.
5. Patrick Zukeran, *Archaeology and the Old Testament* (Probe Ministries International, 2000).
6. John A. Bloom, Contributor, *Evidence for Faith* (Probe Ministries International, 1991), p.173-186. The majority of information in the sub-chapter entitled "Prophecy" was obtained from this source.
7. William J. Cairney, Contributor, *Evidence for Faith* (Probe Ministries International, 1991) p.127-144. The majority of information in the sub-chapter entitled "Microbiology and the Bible" was obtained from this source.
8. F.F. Bruce, *The Canon of Scripture* (InterVarsity Press, 1988) p.231.
9. F.F. Bruce, *History of the Bible in English* (Oxford University Press, 1978), p. 8.
10. Ibid., p. 10.
11. Ibid., p. 33.
12. Ibid., p. 35.
13. Ibid., p. 96.
14. Ibid., p. 101.
15. Ibid., p. 135.
16. Ibid., p. 151.
17. Ibid., p. 186.

18. Ibid., p. 237.
19. Ibid., p. 240.
20. J.W. Hanson, *Universalism: the Prevailing Doctrine* (Universalist Publishing House, 1899), ch.3.
21. Ibid., ch.3
22. Thomas B. Thayer, *The Origin and the History of the Doctrine of Eternal Punishment* (Universalist Publishing House, 1855), ch.3.
23. Hanson, ch. 10.
24. Ibid., ch.10.
25. Ibid., ch.10.
26. *The HarperCollins Bible Dictionary* (HarperCollins Publishers, Inc., 1996), p.102.
27. *Webster's New World Dictionary*, Third College Edition (Simon & Schuster, 1991).

Sources

Albert, David Z. *Quantum Mechanics and Experience*. Harvard University Press, 1992.

Bruce, F.F. *The Canon of Scripture*. InterVarsity Press, 1988.

Bruce, F.F. *History of the Bible in English*. Oxford University Press, 1978.

Cornuke, Robert and Halbrook, David. *In Search of The Mountain of God*. Broadman and Holman Publishers, 2000.

Drosnin, Michael. *The Bible Code*. Simon and Schuster, 1998.

Durant, Will. *The Story of Civilization*. Simon and Schuster, eleven volumes.

Gribbin, John. *In Search of Schrodinger's Cat – Quantum Physics and Reality*. Bantam Books, 1984.

Guillen, Michael. *Five Equations That Changed the World*. Hyperion, 1995.

Hanson, J.W. *Universalism: the Prevailing Doctrine*. Universalist Publishing House, 1899.

HarperCollins Bible Dictionary. HarperCollins Publishers, Inc., 1996.

Johnson, Paul. *A History of Christianity*. Atheneum, 1976.

Johnson, Paul. *A History of the Jews*. HarperPerennial, 1987.

Kafatos, Menas and Nadeau, Robert. *The Conscious Universe: Part and Whole in Modern Physical Theory.* Springer-Verlag, 1990.

Lightfoot, J.B., Harmer, J.R., and Holmes, Michael W. *The Apostolic Fathers.* Baker Book House, 1989.

Montgomery, John Warwick, Editor. *Evidence for Faith.* Probe Ministries International, 1991.

Pamphilus, Eusebius. *Ecclesiastical History.* Baker Book House, 1992.

Penrose, Roger. *Shadows of the Mind.* Oxford University Press, 1994.

Potok, Chaim. *Wanderings.* Fawcett Crest, 1978.

Schuldt, Lynn Louise. *Prophecy Paradox: The Case For A First Century End Time.* Son Mountain Press, 2002.

Smoot, George and Davidson, Keay. *Wrinkles in Time.* William Morrow and Co., Inc., 1993.

Strobel, Lee. *The Case For Christ.* Zondervan Publishing House, 1998.

Thayer, Thomas B. *The Origin and the History of the Doctrine of Eternal Punishment.* Universalist Publishing House, 1855.

Thorne, Kip S. *Black Holes and Time Warps.* W.W. Norton and Co., 1994.

Trefil, James S. *From Atoms to Quarks.* Charles Scribner's Sons, 1980.

Whiston, William. *Josephus.* Kregel Publications, 1981.

Zukeran, Patrick. *Archaeology and the Old Testament.* Probe Ministries International, 2000.

INDEX

A

B

O

P

Q

ABOUT THE AUTHOR

Samuel Graham is an independent biblical and historical researcher who received his education from Miami University, University of Cincinnati, and Northern Kentucky University. Mr. Graham lives with his wife of 29 years in Knoxville, Tennessee. His two adult sons, daughter-in-law, and granddaughter also live in Knoxville.